PERSPECTIVES ON THE *MEMORANDUM*

Perspectives on the *Memorandum*

Policy, practice and research in investigative interviewing

edited by
Helen Westcott
Jocelyn Jones

arena

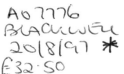
© Helen Westcott and Jocelyn Jones 1997

Published by
Arena
Ashgate Publishing Limited
Gower House
Croft Road
Aldershot
Hants GU11 3HR
England

Ashgate Publishing Company
Old Post Road
Brookfield
Vermont 05036
USA

British Library Cataloguing in Publication Data

Westcott, Helen L.
　Perspectives on the Memorandum
　1. Great Britain. Memorandum of good practice on video
　recorded interviews with child witnesses for criminal
　proceedings
　I. Title　II. Jones, Jocelyn
　345.4'2'075083

　ISBN 1 85742 356 9

Library of Congress Cataloging-in-Publication Data

Perspectives on the memorandum : policy, practice, and research in
　investigative interviewing / edited by Helen Westcott, Jocelyn
　Jones.
　　　p.　cm.
　　Includes bibliographical references and index.
　　ISBN 1-85742-356-9
　　1. Child abuse–Investigation–Great Britain.　2. Interviewing in
　child abuse–Great Britain.　3. Child witnesses–Great Britain.
　I. Westcott, Helen.　II. Jones, Jocelyn.
　HV8079.C46P47　1997
　363.25'95554'0941–dc21
　　　　　　　　　　　　　　　　　　　　　　　　　　　　　97-19596
　　　　　　　　　　　　　　　　　　　　　　　　　　　　　CIP

Phototypeset in Palatino by Raven Typesetters, Chester
Printed in Great Britain by Biddles Ltd, Guildford.

Contents

List of figures and tables

About the authors

Jan Aldridge is Senior Lecturer in Clinical Psychology and Director, Child Forensic Studies at the University of Leeds, and Honorary Consultant Psychologist in Leeds Community and Mental Health Trust. She has developed training initiatives in child psychology and the law with agencies throughout the country, including the police, social services, and the judiciary. She researches and publishes in the area of child witnesses and regularly provides expert evidence to the courts on matters relating to children.

John Brownlow has a background in child protection work with local authorities in London. In 1991, after five years as team manager with the NSPCC in Haringey he became Principal Officer, with lead responsibility for child protection, in Leicestershire. In 1996 he was appointed Area Children's Services Manager for NSPCC East Region.

Tony Butler is Chief Constable of Gloucestershire Constabulary, and is the ACPO representative concerning the *Memorandum*.

Graham Davies is Professor of Psychology at Leicester University. He has extensive experience in researching children's testimony, and has recently evaluated Livelinks and videotaped evidence and the *Memorandum* on behalf of the Home Office.

Liz Davies is a child protection manager, with responsibility for multi-agency training, in an outer London Borough. She qualified in 1972 and has worked as a lecturer in social work and as a generic social worker. Having worked for the London Borough of Islington, she presented evidence through BASW to the recent child abuse inquiries.

Anna Gupta is team manager of a child protection team in a London

Borough social services department. She has considerable multi-cultural experience as a practitioner and manager within busy inner city teams, and recently graduated with an MA in Child Protection Studies from Leicester University.

Enid Hendry is Head of Child Protection Training for the NSPCC. She has a social work background and has been involved in child care training since 1982. She helped develop and run Joint Investigation and Interview Training in Nottinghamshire and has a particular interest in inter-agency training. Her published work includes *Preparing Child Witnesses for Court* (Leicester: NSPCC, 1994) and *Creative Work with Families* (Birmingham: British Association of Social Workers, 1986).

Jocelyn Jones is the Course Director of the post-qualifying Child Protection Studies programme at Leicester University. She has extensive experience in social work practice, management and education. Her research interests centre on the empowerment of child victims, and she has published and presented papers at national and international conferences on this theme. In the field of education and training, she is committed to the development of practitioner research and has developed a national conference and seminar programme to promote research initiatives by practitioners. Jocelyn also writes on current issues in post-qualifying education and training, and is working on the development of competence-based workplace learning and assessment of child protection workers.

Ruth Marchant is development manager and child protection coordinator at Chailey Heritage, a specialist centre for children and young people with physical and multiple disabilities in Sussex. She was one of the consortium of four who produced the ABCD pack – a resource pack on abuse and children who are disabled.

Sarah Nelson is author of *Incest: Fact and Myth* (Edinburgh: Strumullion, 1987), one of the first British feminist analyses of sexual abuse, and has been a regular contributor to conferences on sexual abuse. She is a professional journalist and is currently writing her second book on sexual abuse.

Teresa O'Neill is an experienced guardian *ad litem*. She has recently graduated from Leicester University with an MA in Child Protection Studies, and is currently undertaking research for a PhD at the University of Bristol.

Marcus Page is a senior social work practitioner at the Claremont Child Protection Unit in Brighton, where the multidisciplinary team provides an assessment and therapeutic service for all forms of child abuse. He has written a number of papers on the investigation of sexual abuse and is currently training as a Group-Analytic Psychotherapist.

J.R. Spencer is a Professor of Law at Cambridge University, where his main interest is criminal procedure and evidence. He has written, with Professor Rhona Flin, *The Evidence of Children: The Law and the Psychology* (2nd edition, London: Blackstone Press, 1993.) He has travelled widely, frequently lecturing in universities in France.

Amanda Wade is currently studying at the University of Leeds, where she is completing a doctoral thesis on the child witness and the criminal justice process. She previously worked in the personal social services as a practitioner and manager.

Brian Waller has been Director of Social Services in Leicestershire since 1988, and is currently Chair of the Children and Families Committee of the Association of Directors of Social Services (ADSS). He has recently been elected as Junior Vice President of the Association and will assume the post of President of the ADSS in 1998. Brian is associated with a number of voluntary organisations and is an adviser to the Association of County Councils and the Prince's Trust.

Helen Westcott is Lecturer in Psychology at The Open University. She was previously Research Officer with the NSPCC in London, and has studied many aspects of children's testimony for a number of years. She has trained and published widely on this and related areas, including children's experiences of social work intervention and the abuse of disabled children.

J. Clare Wilson is Senior Lecturer in Psychology at the University of South Australia, Adelaide. Until recently, she was a Lecturer at the Department of Psychology, Leicester University, where, with Professor Graham Davies she evaluated videotaped evidence and the *Memorandum* on behalf of the Home Office.

Preface

Several busy years have passed since the *Memorandum of Good Practice on Video Recorded Interviews with Child Witnesses* was implemented by the Home Office in October 1992. Busy, because of the phenomenal number of video-taped interviews that have taken place in that period, and because of the continuing changes in service delivery within the personal social services. Witness, for example, the 'knock-on' effects of the government's policy shift in child protection heralded by publication of *Messages from Research* in 1995. Given the extent of activity in this field, we saw this book as an opportunity to step back and evaluate the *Memorandum* and its impact.

In order to facilitate a comprehensive evaluation of the *Memorandum*, a deliberately mixed group of professionals was approached to provide chapters. Academics and practitioners do not often appear side by side in textbooks, but we deliberately sought such an alliance here in order to ensure that a whole spectrum of perspectives is presented, and to provoke debate. With such a controversial document as the *Memorandum*, we felt that multi-disciplinary assessment offers the only way forward. In providing such a wide-ranging set of chapters, our aim has also been to ensure that the broader practice context within which the *Memorandum* operates is made clear. We want this book to be practically useful as well as provocative.

As editors we have therefore deliberately not exercised the 'red pen' when different authors have offered a clash of perspectives, or when the same set of research findings have been interpreted in a variety of ways. For the reader, we hope such differences will perhaps act as a catalyst for assessing the *Memorandum* in new ways. To this end, it is worth repeating the opening statement of the *Memorandum*'s foreword here so that readers can consider it in the light of the various issues raised throughout the book: 'The interests of justice and the interests of the child are not alternatives.'

Layout of the book

The book consists of 13 chapters, and the first four 'set the scene' through the presentation of perspectives from the professional standpoint. Graham Davies and Clare Wilson (Chapter 1) start by offering an overview of implementation of the *Memorandum*, based on the research they conducted on behalf of the Home Office (Davies et al., 1995). They conclude on an upbeat note about the *Memorandum* and its implementation, though noting the need to refine and develop its recommendations. This provides a useful starting point to which subsequent chapters can be compared.

In Chapter 2, John Brownlow and Brian Waller then draw on their particular experiences in Leicestershire Social Services Department, as well as the national picture from the Association of Directors of Social Services, to offer a social services perspective. A number of practical implementation problems are highlighted, as well as the real difficulty for social workers in defining their role in relation to the *Memorandum*, and the continuing 'Section 17 vs Section 47' debate.

In Chapter 3, Tony Butler presents the police view of the *Memorandum*. Again a number of operational difficulties are outlined, but a more positive view of the *Memorandum*'s implementation emerges. Tony concludes that the issues of training standards, child witness preparation and guidance to judges and counsel remain to be addressed in order for the benefits of the *Memorandum* to be built upon.

Teresa O'Neill (Chapter 4) then presents an analysis of the implications of the *Memorandum* for investigations where civil public law proceedings are instigated, and a guardian *ad litem* appointed. Conflicts between the criminal and civil courts, and their implications for children and guardians are discussed. She concludes that guardians must see themselves as advocates for children who are powerless in the adult world of the courts.

Chapters 5 through 7 change emphasis to explicitly consider children's perspectives. Amanda Wade and Helen Westcott (Chapter 5) first draw upon their own and existing research to highlight the *Memorandum*'s failure to properly address issues for child witnesses. Verbatim material from children and young people is used to illustrate how children are effectively disempowered by the interview process from planning to execution.

Ruth Marchant and Marcus Page (Chapter 6) then discuss the particular requirements of disabled children undergoing *Memorandum* interviews. This chapter will be especially welcomed by practitioners working in this area, since the authors provide much advice on how *Memorandum* interviews may be approached to include disabled children. The social and political context is also discussed.

Black children and the *Memorandum* are discussed by Anna Gupta in Chapter 7. Initially, the social and political context is outlined, particularly with respect to manifestations of racism. Again, practitioners will find the detailed consideration of additional factors to be addressed in *Memorandum* interviews arising from the child's racial and cultural background a valuable resource.

The next four chapters examine different aspects of the broader context in which the *Memorandum* is operating. John Spencer (Chapter 8) first provides an international overview of alternative measures for dealing with children's evidence, as well as reviewing the much neglected issue of the European Convention on Human Rights in relation to the Criminal Justice Act 1991 and the *Memorandum*.

In Chapter 9, Liz Davies then considers alternative models of working in investigations of organised abuse. She proposes a change of approach so that the emphasis is placed on the perpetrator, and *Memorandum* interviews comprise only one part of a variety of measures used to curtail offenders' activities. Of foremost importance is the establishment of local, regional and national joint investigation teams.

In Chapter 10, Jan Aldridge discusses the steps necessary after a *Memorandum* interview to prepare children for court. She highlights the varying sources of stress for children caught up in the legal system, including their many real fears, and describes how preparation work can ameliorate these stressors to the benefit of the child and their evidence.

Dilemmas and opportunities in training around the *Memorandum* are raised by Enid Hendry and Jocelyn Jones in Chapter 11. Their chapter provides an analysis of oppression and power relationships, central but frequently neglected issues to be addressed in joint training, and goes on to offer concrete and practical examples of how training programmes can address these crucial issues.

The final two chapters provide overviews of issues relating to the *Memorandum*. First, Sarah Nelson (Chapter 12) offers a wide-ranging critique from a child-centred perspective. While supporting selective use of video-taped interviews with child witnesses, she questions whether children's evidence has to remain central to child abuse prosecutions. Instead, she calls for a shift by all agencies towards the investigation of suspected adults.

Finally, in Chapter 13 we close with a review of the *Memorandum* in the light of preceding chapters. We critically examine the *Memorandum*'s achievements to date in relation to protecting children, and question what a 'right to justice' actually means for children. In considering the 'way ahead', we conclude that a dual approach is necessary which combines immediate changes with a fundamental review of the way in which children's evidence is obtained. Empowerment of children at both personal and structural levels is seen as essential.

Note on presentation

Before leaving readers to explore the book, a brief note on presentation is required. First, the term 'children' has been used throughout to denote children and young people up to the age of 18 years, unless otherwise stated by authors. Secondly, where authors have provided case examples or quotations, names and non-essential details have been changed to maintain confidentiality.

Helen Westcott and Jocelyn Jones

Reference

Davies, G., Wilson, C., Mitchell, R. and Milson, J. (1995) *Videotaping Children's Evidence: An Evaluation*, London: HMSO.

1 Implementation of the *Memorandum*: an overview

Graham Davies and Clare Wilson

The introduction of the *Memorandum of Good Practice on Video Recorded Interviews with Child Witnesses for Criminal Proceedings* (Home Office, 1992) formed part of a general review of the rules governing the reception of evidence by children at court. In the opinion of many police officers and social workers that review is far from complete (Davies and Wilson, 1994; Social Services Inspectorate, 1994). The motive for change was the belated realisation, on the one hand, of the scale of physical and sexual abuse in our society and, on the other hand, that children can be reliable witnesses, given appropriate questioning and legal procedures that take account of their age and vulnerability (Goodman, 1984; Goodman and Helgeson, 1985). This change in attitude has been reflected in alterations to the law that have done away with the formal obstacles to the hearing of children's evidence such as the competency test, the corroboration requirement and the special caution from the judge to the jury in cases involving children's evidence (Spencer and Flin, 1993). The Criminal Justice and Public Order Act 1994 spells out the view explicitly that courts should normally be prepared to listen to the evidence of children and juries should decide what weight to attach to it.

Hand in hand with alterations to the law have come changes in criminal procedure designed to make the giving of evidence by children less stressful. Research in both Britain (Flin et al., 1988) and the United States (Parker, 1982; Goodman, 1984) has demonstrated that concerns about facing the accused while tendering evidence and the abnormal nature of the court experience are major impediments to the involvement of children in the criminal courts. The Criminal Justice Act 1988 sought to address these concerns by permitting for the first time children in criminal cases to give their evidence from outside the courtroom and have their testimony relayed to the court via closed-circuit television (the 'live link'). If operated appropriately, this meant that the child need never see the accused or enter the courtroom during the reception of their evidence. An evaluation of these new procedures commissioned by the

1

Home Office (Davies and Noon, 1991) found widespread acceptance of the 'live link' among judges, barristers and court officials. Recent figures provided by Plotnikoff and Woolfson (personal communication) suggest that 64 per cent of all child witnesses give their evidence via the 'live link', 25 per cent do so live in court in the traditional way while a further 11 per cent give their evidence in court protected by screens.

The report by Davies and Noon (1991) pointed out that while the 'live link' provision assisted children in giving their evidence, significant difficulties still remained for many children. In particular, examination by a barrister at court remained a traumatic and baffling experience, particularly for younger witnesses. In all, only 8 per cent of the children who used the link were under eight years of age. There were also frequently long delays between a suspect being charged and the case coming to court. Davies and Noon reported an average delay in cases of child sexual abuse of some 21 months, a figure remaining unchanged despite innovations designed to accelerate the processing of cases involving children (Plotnikoff and Woolfson, 1995). Such long delays have inevitable consequences in the quality of children's evidence and its freshness of detail (Flin et al., 1993).

One answer to these problems would be to use videotaped interviews between the child and a supportive interviewer, recorded soon after the allegations were made, and to show this videotape to the court. Such a proposal was recommended by the Pigot Committee which had been set up by the Home Office to consider the feasibility of such a scheme.

The Pigot Committee's report (Home Office, 1989) endorsed the value of tape recorded interviews in criminal trials involving children. If recordings were made at an early stage of the investigation, then the court would have a fresh account of the alleged incident, untarnished by subsequent interviews or the passage of time. The existence of such an interview would minimise the need for multiple interviews or the child's appearance at preliminary hearings. The interview would be conducted by police officers and social workers cooperating in the spirit of the *Working Together* report (Department of Health, 1991). Pigot recognised the special nature of these interviews in that they were simultaneously investigative and evidential. He recommended that they be governed by a code of practice to ensure their acceptability to the criminal courts. Pigot proposed that such interviews be played at court as a substitute for the traditional live examination of the child by the prosecuting counsel. The report went on to suggest that the principle of prior videotaping might also be extended to cover the child's cross-examination by the defence barrister to be conducted in the presence of the judge in an informal setting which would be less intimidating for the child.

While Pigot's proposals received broad endorsement from child protection agencies and some lawyers (see Spencer, 1991), there was considerable resistance within the Home Office to embracing the total Pigot 'package'.

Instead, the Criminal Justice Act 1991 permitted videotaped interviews to be substituted for the child's examination-in-chief at court but the child still had to be present for cross-examination on the day of the trial. The core of the report regarding the importance of interviewing style resulted from a survey of research and best practice commissioned from a psychologist and a lawyer (Bull, 1995). This evolved via a series of revisions, guided by a working party of concerned professionals, into the *Memorandum*. The philosophy of the *Memorandum* was that as far as possible, children should tell their own story assisted by prompts and questions of gradually increasing explicitness: the so-called 'phased interview'. The publication also contained advice on technical aspects of the interviews and legal issues surrounding questioning.

It was recognised that the introduction of the *Memorandum* had training implications for the police officers and social workers involved in interviewing and familiarity training was required for senior police officers and managers. In preparation for the implementation of the Act in October 1992, the police began 'trickle-down' training based at Hendon Police College whereby groups of staff received training on the *Memorandum* in anticipation that those trainees in turn would pass on their knowledge at a local level. By all accounts, these early attempts at training revealed sharply discrepant interpretations of certain key elements of the *Memorandum* and were not perceived by participants as greatly encouraging: 'It was the only police course I have ever been on where the trainees founded a survivors' group' (anonymous police officer).

Social workers awaited the special training pack developed by The Open University which, for a variety of reasons, did not become available until February 1993. The Open University pack is now used in some form by most local authorities (Social Services Inspectorate, 1994), though it has been criticised by some police officers as being too rudimentary (Hughes et al., 1996).

An evaluation concerning the first two years of the *Memorandum*'s implementation was commissioned by the Home Office from the authors at Leicester University (Davies et al., 1995). The remit of the research team covered the views of professionals using the new procedure (social workers, police officers, barristers and judges), observational studies of the quality and impact of the evidence of children via videotape (as opposed to live at court) and an audit of a sample of taped interviews to establish the degree to which they followed the recommendations of the *Memorandum*. In addition, the Lord Chancellor's Department made available statistics on the frequency and outcomes of trials to try to establish the impact of the new provisions on verdicts. In contrast to the earlier research on live links, permission was also given to approach the child witnesses, allowing the children to express their own reaction to the new legislation.

Attitudes of child protection and legal professionals

The views of professionals were surveyed twice: in February 1993 prior to experience with the Act to assess hopes and concerns, and again in August 1994 to assess how expectations had been borne out with experience. All participants were asked to identify the advantages and the disadvantages for the child and the criminal justice system of the new legislation. For ease of analysis, the various professional groups were divided in two: the child protection group (police and social workers) and the court group (barristers and judges). The numbers of professionals who responded to the surveys are presented in Table 1.1.

Table 1.1   The number of respondents and the number of questionnaires distributed to the four professions surveyed

Profession	Questionnaire type	Number of respondents	Number distributed
Judge	Preliminary	15	15
Judge	Post	17	17
Barrister	Preliminary	41	100
Barrister	Post	61	200
Police	Preliminary	117	200
Police	Post	76	200
Social worker	Preliminary	75	400
Social worker	Post	42	500

Turning to the views of the child protection workers, there was nearly unanimous support for the introduction of videotaped evidence and for the *Memorandum*. However, the majority had little confidence that the current form of the Act would be in the interest of justice or the child: many believed that the court experience would remain a major source of trauma over and above the original abuse. They saw the primary advantage of the new legislation as being the reduction of stress at court for the child while the major disadvantage was the continuing need for the child to undergo live cross-examination. One of the major concerns for the child protection professionals was the need for adequate training and supervision.

When child protection professionals who had experience of the new legislation were surveyed, their enthusiasm for the *Memorandum* and the principles of videotaped interviews was undiminished, but certain practical difficulties in the operation of the Act had begun to emerge. In particular, social workers complained that the interviews were too frequently led by police officers with the result that social workers felt deskilled and divorced from the investigative process. These fears are supported by the findings of the Social Services Inspectorate Survey (1994) which reported that police officers normally led interviews in 75 per cent of the local authorities surveyed compared to 8 per cent in which social workers led the interviews. There were also concerns expressed by the social workers that the evidence-gathering function of the interviews was overshadowing the therapeutic needs of the child.

The survey also showed that while anxieties about training had diminished, just under half the respondents felt that training could be improved or made a continuing process. Scepticism as to whether the existing version of the Act was in the best interests of the child or the criminal justice system was maintained, with a minority calling for the implementation of the Pigot Report in full.

Turning to the views of the court professionals, the preliminary survey suggested a much more muted response to the main features of the new legislation, particularly among barristers. Only 40 per cent of barristers were in favour of the videotaping of evidence or the *Memorandum*: the primary concern being that inadequacies in interviewing would permit false allegations to go undetected. Judges generally took a more positive view on these points but as such a small sample of the judiciary took part, one should be cautious in interpreting their results. The court professionals shared the child protection professionals' view that a reduction in stress for the child was the principle advantage.

When the court professionals were surveyed after experience with the Act, the already muted enthusiasm for its provision had declined further, although 75 per cent of the select group of judges believed it was working in the interests of the child. A reduction in stress for the witness was still seen as the principle advantage. However, this was qualified by an increasing concern among prosecution barristers that videotaped evidence had less impact on the jury. The defence barristers continued to be concerned that lying was going undetected while both groups (32 per cent of prosecution and 43 per cent of defence barristers) expressed concerns that children who gave their evidence via videotape might be unprepared for the rigours of cross-examination.

Evaluation of a sample of taped interviews

The views of lawyers and judges on the quality of the videotapes they had seen was somewhat mixed: just over half of both groups felt the tapes generally complied with the rules of evidence, though the proportion agreeing among the defence was somewhat lower. In order to gauge the degree to which videotapes were being made in accordance with the recommendations of the *Memorandum*, a sample of 40 interviews was systematically evaluated by the research team. The tapes came from six different police forces and permission to view the tapes was secured from the interviewers, the children and their carers. None of the tapes sampled had been used in a criminal trial. All interviews were police led (90 per cent by a female officer) and involved 26 female and 14 male witnesses, none of whom were from ethnic minorities or had special needs.

The *Memorandum* advocates an interview with four phases: rapport building, free narrative from the child, questioning from the interviewer and a closure phase. In the sample, rapport lasted an average of 7 minutes (with a maximum of 30 minutes). Sometimes it appeared that the rapport stage was being extended as much to overcome the interviewer's nervousness as that of the child's. In 30 per cent of the interviews, the interviewer established that the child understood the difference between truth and lies. However, the reminder that 'don't know' responses were acceptable was frequently missing.

Free narrative was the only stage not found with any frequency in interviews: some 28 per cent of tapes examined lacked this stage. The omission is a significant one, given the proportionately higher accuracy of spontaneous statements relative to those elicited by questioning (Dent and Stephenson, 1979), and the advantage to the court of hearing the allegations in the child's own words. One reason for the lack of free narrative may have been that the interview itself was either unnecessary (nothing untoward had occurred, so there was nothing to report) or premature (i.e., the child was not yet ready to talk to a stranger about abusive events). However, in other instances, interviewers were over-eager to ask the child questions before he or she had finished speaking: a problem also encountered among police interviewers of adult witnesses (Fisher and Geiselman, 1992). Some 43 per cent of interviewers were judged to have needlessly rushed children through the free narrative phase: the average time taken for this phase of the interview was less than two minutes.

During the questioning phase, some 30 per cent of interviews were judged to have progressed from open-ended to closed questions and of the latter too many were judged to be answerable by the child saying 'yes' or 'no'. Such questions tend to involve the interviewer formulating an hypothesis which is then put to the child for confirmation, and such questions have been a prime source of misinformation in some celebrated miscarriages of justice in child abuse investigations (Ceci and Bruck, 1995).

The final phase of closure also took less than three minutes on average. At worst, some interviewers simply got up and left the room, but 35 per cent of interviewers allowed children the opportunity to ask questions of them about the nature and purpose of the interview. A further 28 per cent used this phase to ask about truth and lies. Some police officers considered this a good tactic as it allowed the jury to see the children strongly declare the truthfulness of their statement. However, the reason children make such a strong declaration at this point in the interview may well be due to their perceiving the question as querying the veracity of their previous statements, and so such questioning post-disclosure may not be in the best interests of the child.

Technically, it was evident that the police and local authorities had spent money wisely on a high standard of equipment which gave effective sound and picture quality. The *Memorandum* recommendations had generally been followed, but some technical problems remained. While the interviewer was invariably audible, in approximately one-quarter of all interviews, the child could barely be heard. The use of noisy play objects such as crayons and beanbags or external noise was a problem on some tapes. The major difficulty with the picture was that the child was not always clearly in vision in nearly half the tapes. The common use of a sofa to seat both the interviewer and the child was a frequent cause of difficulty: future editions of the *Memorandum* should include arrangements where children can face the camera rather than be placed sideways on, which can lead to their being blotted out by the insert designed to show the complete room (Davies et al., 1995).

However, such detailed criticism should not mask the overall positive view which emerges from observation of the tapes. A clear account was assessed as having been obtained in as many as 75 per cent of all interviews and 70 per cent of children were judged to be relaxed. Moreover, without exception, interviewers were judged to be communicating in language appropriate to the age of the child, a marked contrast to that used frequently by barristers in the courtroom (Davies and Noon, 1991). The feedback from the small sample of children ($n = 17$) who agreed to give their views on the interviewing experience were also positive in 65 per cent of cases.

The *Memorandum* in court

All four professional groups surveyed had expressed the hope that videotaped interviews would reduce the stress of a court appearance for the child. The research supports this, at least as regards the prosecution's examination of the child's evidence. A total of 150 children were observed giving evidence in court of which 110 (73 per cent) gave their evidence in the form of a videotaped interview. Ratings of the two modes of testimony suggested that children giving evidence live at court were significantly more anxious than those giving evidence in a pre-recorded interview. The explanation for this difference may lie in the greater supportiveness of the child protection interviewers: 72 per cent of the latter were rated as supportive compared to 54 per cent of prosecution barristers. Moreover, videotaped interviewers were significantly more likely to adjust their style of speaking to the age of the child. Only in audibility did the evidence received at court via the live link score over pre-recorded interviews. However, both groups of witnesses were judged to have given their evidence in an effective manner: 84 per cent of those interviewed on videotape and 79 per cent of those examined at court were rated as successful in this regard.

Social workers and police officers expressed concern that while the videotape may reduce stress for the child, the child would be unprepared to deal with cross-examination. The court observers' perceptions of stress and mood failed to support the assumption that children who had not been 'warmed up' by the prosecution's questioning would be more distressed. However, such a result needs to be treated with caution given the high levels of anxiety noted in both groups of witnesses.

A concern voiced by both judges and barristers was that the actual quality of interviewing conducted by the child professionals would be inadequate. Data from the Lord Chancellor's Department do not support the view that the tapes which are submitted at court are evidentially flawed. Between 1 October 1992 and 30 June 1994, some 640 applications were made to show videotaped interviews as part of the criminal proceedings and of these 470 were granted. However, only 25 of non-approved applications were rejected for evidential reasons, the remainder were overtaken by late guilty pleas from the accused and the applications therefore became redundant.

Of course, the application to show a video does not guarantee that it will be shown. Of the 470 applications granted, only 202 were definitely known to have been shown in court. Of the remainder, as many as one in four were withdrawn by the prosecution, frequently on the day of the trial. This behaviour by the prosecution often reflected a prime concern of the barristers surveyed – that the impact of the video on the jury would be less than the child's live testimony at court. Further, the prosecution barrister is often replaced between committal and trial. Children caught up in such cases suffer a double jeopardy: not only have they been led to believe it will not be necessary to give live evidence in court only to be disillusioned on the day of trial, but also they have been deprived of the opportunity to view their videotape prior to testifying. It is not surprising then that in the 25 court cases attended by observers where a switch from video to live evidence was made, 12 trials broke down within minutes of the child taking the stand because of the child's difficulty in following the barristers' questions.

As to the final concern of the legal professionals, that children involved in *Memorandum* interviews will find it easier to lie, research to date can produce no clear answer. However, a number of findings point in the opposing direction. For instance, if children were lying regularly in *Memorandum* interviews, then one might expect that the accused person would be more likely to plead not guilty when faced with videotaped evidence than conventional statements. However, the rate of guilty pleas where video interviews are present is, if anything, higher (49 per cent late guilty pleas) than in cases where no *Memorandum* interview has been made (44 per cent). Further, if defence counsel has done their job and exposed lying children, one might expect jury convictions to be substantially lower in trials featuring *Memorandum* interviews than in more conventional trials. Again, the results show convictions in trials containing *Memorandum* interviews (48 per cent) were not significantly lower than for live examinations (43 per cent).

It is evident that the worst fears of both child protection professionals and legal professionals have not been born out by experience of the Act in practice. Interviews conducted according to the principles of the *Memorandum* are being admitted on a regular basis into the criminal court and securing convictions for child sexual abuse. The use of *Memorandum* interviews has gone from being the exception to being the norm: by June 1994, 75 per cent of all sexual abuse cases were accompanied by applications to show a videotape.

However, that does not mean that there are not still serious areas of concern with the existing legislation. While the quality of those interviews that reach court seemed generally high, they represented only a small minority of the number of videotapes actually made. A survey by Butler (Association of Chief Police Officers, 1993) suggested that police forces in England and Wales had conducted nearly 15,000 interviews under the terms of the *Memorandum* in the first nine months of the legislation, of which only 152 had resulted in an application to show the video at court. While the numbers of interviews leading to criminal proceedings has generally increased since the Butler survey, the results do suggest that very large numbers of interviews were being conducted to little apparent purpose. Not surprisingly perhaps, there have been calls for social workers to withdraw from investigative interviewing on the grounds that scarce resources would be better deployed in the more traditional role of child protection (Waller, 1995).

However, it is far from clear whether a way back to their traditional role is available to social workers. The events at Cleveland and elsewhere prior to the 1991 Act indicated a need for a document akin to the *Memorandum* to govern the questioning of all children by social workers (Department of Health and Social Security, 1988). Having established the value of videotaping as a contemporaneous record, it seems unlikely that many local authorities would wish to return to hearsay and scribbled notes. More productive interviewing and continuing refinement and development of the *Memorandum* may be the effective way forward.

When the *Memorandum* was first published it was envisaged that, like the Highway Code to which it is sometimes compared, it would be subject to periodic revision. The Leicester research (Davies et al., 1995) has drawn attention to a number of areas of ambiguity or shortcomings within the document, and those have been reinforced more recently by calls for action by such organisations as the National Society for the Prevention of Cruelty to Children (NSPCC) (Davies and Wilson, 1996). In particular, more explicit guidelines are required on pre-interview practice. For example, should children be evidentially interviewed if they are not prepared and/or not able to give a full and frank account of the abuse they have suffered? Greater clarification of what is and what is not permissible in preliminary discussions would help to reduce the number of unproductive interviews to the benefit of all concerned. Other issues in need of clarification and extension mentioned by the respondents in the Leicester study include the need to take account of the particular difficulties of very young children and of those with special needs. There was also no information available to the researchers regarding children from ethnic minorities – at what rate do they report abuse, are interviews being conducted with them and, if so, what happens to them? The Leicester researchers did not observe any such cases reaching court.

Concern surrounding the appropriate training of interviewers in *Memorandum* procedures was acute among the child protection professionals surveyed in the Leicester research and has continued to be a major issue. The decision of many social work departments to spread training thinly but widely among staff, compared to the more concentrated training of specialised teams by most police forces, has led to a disparity of experience which may explain why the majority of interviews are led by police officers (Social Services Inspectorate, 1994). Several years after the introduction of the *Memorandum* there are still differences in interpretation of its recommendations at a local level and no agreed national curriculum or accreditation system (Hughes et al., 1996). A recent research award from the Police Research Group to the authors will evaluate the viability of a national scheme of training for police officers involved in child protection work.

The Leicester research demonstrates the wide acceptance of the principles of the *Memorandum* among all groups, with the pointed exception of barristers. It is also of interest that many concerns of the various professional groups were not born out by the data, suggesting the importance of objective research to help inform those professionals working in this area. The *Memorandum* provides safeguards for the child, the interviewers and the accused which are unlikely to be readily surrendered. The research demonstrated that the *Memorandum* is a useful tool in the legitimate prosecution of child sex offenders. It is in the interests of all parties to refine and develop its recommendations to ensure that it is more widely and effectively employed in the interests of justice and children.

References

Association of Chief of Police Officers (1993), *Survey of the Use of Videotaped Interviews with Child Witnesses by Police Forces in England and Wales,* Cheltenham: Gloucestershire Constabulary.

Bull, R. (1995), 'Good practice for video recorded interviews with child witnesses for use in criminal proceedings', in G. Davies, S. Lloyd-Bostock, M. McMurran and C. Wilson (eds) *Psychology, Law and Criminal Justice,* Berlin: De Gruyter.

Ceci, S.J. and Bruck, M. (1995), *Jeopardy in the Courtroom: A Scientific Analysis of Children's Testimony,* Washington, DC: American Psychological Association.

Davies, G.M. and Noon, E. (1991), *An Evaluation of the Live Link for Child Witnesses,* London: Home Office.

Davies, G.M. and Wilson, J.C. (1994), 'The videotaping of children's evidence: issues of research and practice', *Practitioners' Child Law Bulletin,* 23, 68–70.

Davies, G.M. and Wilson, J.C. (1996), 'Child witnesses: three years on', *Forensic Update,* 46, 20–2.

Davies, G.M., Wilson, J.C., Mitchell, R. and Milsom, J. (1995), *Videotaping Children's Evidence: An Evaluation,* London: HMSO.

Dent, H. and Stephenson, G. (1979), 'An experimental study of the effectiveness of different techniques of questioning child witnesses,' *British Journal of Social and Clinical Psychology,* 18, 45–51.

Department of Health (1991), *Working Together Under the Children Act 1989 – A Guide to the Arrangements for Interagency Co-operation for the Protection of Children from Abuse,* London: HMSO.

Department of Health and Social Security (1988), *Report of the Inquiry into Child Abuse in Cleveland 1987 (Cm412),* The Butler–Sloss Report, London: HMSO.

Fisher, R. and Geiselman, E. (1992), *Memory-Enhancing Techniques for Investigative Interviewing: The Cognitive Interview,* Springfield, IL: C.C. Thomas.

Flin, R., Bull, R., Boon, J. and Knox, A. (1993), 'Child witnesses in Scottish criminal trials', *International Review of Victimology,* 2, 319–39.

Flin, R.H., Davies G., and Tarrant, A. (1988), *The Child Witness.* Final Report to the Scottish Home and Health Department. Grant 85/9290. Aberdeen: Robert Gordon's Institute of Technology.

Goodman, G.S. (1984), 'The child witness: conclusions and future directions for research and legal practice', *Journal of Social Issues,* 40, 157–75.

Goodman, G.S. and Helgeson, V.S. (1985), 'Child sexual assault: children's memory and the law', *University of Miami Law Review,* 40, 181–208.

Home Office (1989), *Report of the Advisory Group on Video Evidence,* chairman Judge Thomas Pigot QC, London: Home Office.

Home Office and Department of Health (1992), *Memorandum of Good Practice on Video Recorded Interviews with Child Witnesses for Criminal Proceedings*, London: HMSO.

Hughes, B., Parker, H. and Gallagher, B. (1996), *Policing Child Sexual Abuse: The View from Police Practitioners*, London: Home Office.

Open University/Department of Health and Social Welfare (1993), *Investigative Interviewing with Children: Trainers' Pack K501*, Dorset: Blackmore.

Parker, J. (1982), 'The rights of child witnesses: is the court a protector or perpetrator?', *New England Law Review*, 17, 643–717.

Plotnikoff, J. and Woolfson, R. (1995), *Prosecuting Child Abuse: An Evaluation of the Government's Speedy Progress Policy*, London: Blackstone.

Social Services Inspectorate (1994), *The Child, the Court and the Video*, London: Department of Health.

Spencer, J.R. (1991), 'Reformers despair', *New Law Journal*, 141, 787.

Spencer, J.R. and Flin, R. (1993), *The Evidence of Children* (2nd edn), London: Blackstone.

Waller, B. (1995), 'The hidden trial of child victims', *Guardian*, Society section, 25 January, p. 2.

2 The *Memorandum*: a social services perspective

John Brownlow and Brian Waller

This chapter offers a critical commentary on the process of introducing video recorded interviews and on their effectiveness in practice from the perspective of a local authority social services department. We look at the experience of one local authority in implementing the *Memorandum of Good Practice on Video Recorded Interviews with Child Witnesses for Criminal Proceedings* (Home Office, 1992) and contrast this with the national surveys and debate on the value of the new arrangements. We concentrate primarily on practice in the field and on the frameworks for policy and practice guiding video recording and upon its effects on children and professionals.

We suggest that the guidelines for video recording interviews, introduced in 1992, have become a central influence in the debate currently affecting child care services; and the evaluation of these arrangements cannot be divorced from the argument about what constitutes the task of social workers and the way in which their responsibilities are to be exercised in the latter part of the 1990s.

Wattam (1992) argues that, in following the guidelines for video recording contained in the *Memorandum*, social workers have become absorbed in a system in which the requirements of the criminal justice system predominate. She contrasts the *Memorandum*, in which evidential requirements of the criminal investigation are the prime consideration, with the Children Act principle that the welfare of the child is paramount. There is research evidence (Davies et al., 1995) to suggest that the introduction of the *Memorandum* has improved interviewing techniques and that they now have more value for evidential purposes. However, the development of the existing arrangements for joint investigation between police and social services has pulled social workers ever further into the process of gathering forensic evidence for the purpose of the criminal investigation. Wendy Rose, a senior official with the Social Services Inspectorate, told a meeting of child protection coordinators in 1995 that in her view social work has 'lost its way' and that the social

13

welfare needs of the child and family are being neglected; a position based upon *Messages From Research* (Department of Health, 1995). Furthermore, national surveys and local evidence suggest that the proportion of video recordings used in court is tiny, raising significant questions about the practice and cost-effectiveness of the new arrangements.

Background

The report on events in Cleveland in 1988 and the judgement on the Rochdale case given in open court by Mr Justice Brown in 1991 highlighted both the sensitivity and complexity of investigation and assessment of child sexual abuse. In both cases there was considerable criticism from the judiciary about the quality of interviewing and lack of video evidence. This raised expectations that social services should offer video evidence in civil proceedings, particularly in the High Court, but these expectations were never put into national guidance in any coherent form. Instead, social workers were routinely asked in the witness box whether they had read the *Cleveland Report* (DHSS, 1988); a question of doubtful value given the paucity of practical detail about video recording or interview techniques contained within it. Likewise, the Rochdale judgement, while frequently referred to, was never published in a form which permitted widespread circulation within social services departments.

Prompted by concern about the difficulty in obtaining convictions in child sexual abuse cases and about the way in which child witnesses were treated in court, the findings of the Pigot Report (Home Office, 1989) were generally welcomed. However, there was widespread dismay that they were not fully implemented and concern that children would still have to be available in court for live cross-examination.

The subsequent publication of the *Memorandum* in 1992 led to a great deal of national and local activity, with social services, police and Area Child Protection Committees establishing resources, procedures and training. The *Memorandum* provided a great deal in the way of detail about how interviews were to be conducted but little guidance on the associated procedural framework which would be needed or when interviews should be conducted. As a consequence each social services department and police force was left to establish its own arrangements and, importantly, its own training programme. This led in some areas to strains in relations between the two agencies as they tried to formulate joint policy which reflected the inevitably different priorities of each. As a consequence, there have been inconsistencies in the application of the new arrangements across the country, as borne out in the evaluation programmes sponsored by the Home Office (Davies et al., 1995) and the Department of Health (1994).

Implementation in Leicestershire

As in most other areas, the local situation prior to the introduction of the *Memorandum* was confused. There was a widespread reluctance to video record interviews as a matter of routine because of worries about the quality of equipment, lack of facilities, interviewing skills, and the possible negative impact on the child. However, in the course of a complex network abuse case in the High Court in 1991 the social services department faced judicial criticism for not providing video evidence, the judge making specific reference to the ruling in the Rochdale case. As a result, the local authority solicitors advised that the department should video record interviews in all sexual abuse cases where care proceedings were considered likely, particularly in the more complex cases which might end up in the High Court.

The police were understandably very reluctant to become involved in video recorded interviews in advance of the publication of the *Memorandum*. Fortunately, few such circumstances arose in the period prior to publication in 1992.

Local implementation of the *Memorandum* was delayed while the police established a specialist unit for dealing with child protection cases. This led to a degree of tension, with social services under pressure from its legal advisers. A joint working group was established which included representatives of police, social services, the Crown Prosecution Service (CPS) and specialist advisers. This group developed a framework for training, the establishment of video facilities, local guidance on when to make a video recording and the storage and disposal of tapes.

The decision to conduct a video recorded interview

The issue of whether to video record an interview was identified at an early stage as being of key importance. The *Memorandum* states that, 'once it has become clear that a criminal offence may have been committed an interview should be arranged, as soon as is practicable'(para. 1.9). The range of offences in which video recording of child witnesses is permitted is very wide, including most violent or sexual offences. The *Memorandum* could therefore be taken to imply that a video recording could (or should) be made in all situations where there is good reason to suspect that a child has been abused, whether physically or sexually. This is clearly impracticable and so local guidelines were developed which attempted to establish criteria for when to video record an interview.

In the process of drafting a protocol, differences in agency approach emerged. The police tended to regard video recording simply as 'best evidence' and as a more convenient way to record the interview than taking contemporaneous notes and compiling a statement. Many social workers took a more cautious approach. Some of this initial caution could be attributed to a lack of confidence in 'performing' in front of a camera and unfamiliarity with the technology, and was dealt with by training and experience. Other concerns, about the child's welfare and about the role of the social worker in the investigative process, have remained harder to tackle.

As a result of their different perspective, the police tended to want to record more interviews than their social services colleagues. Social services representatives argued that conducting unnecessary interviews would be wasteful of resources and might cause children undue distress. It was therefore decided that, in line with the *Memorandum*, a joint decision should be made in each case by both agencies on the basis of agreed criteria.

The *Memorandum* acknowledges that it may not be clear at the outset whether a criminal investigation is required and states that, 'it is possible that some initial questioning may have taken place before the police are involved' (para. 1.8). This was considered locally to be inadequate and that some test was needed of whether the child had something significant to say. The local protocol, agreed by the Leicestershire police and social services (Leicestershire Constabulary, 1993), stated that: 'video recorded interviews should normally only be conducted after it has been established that a child wishes to speak about an allegation of abuse. Therefore in some cases a preliminary interview may be necessary which is not video recorded.'

Having established the need for an interview, the expressed intention is to record all interviews where sexual abuse is alleged, cases involving network/organised abuse and some cases of serious injury. The following criteria were also agreed as considerations in determining whether or not to make a video recorded interview:

- the child's wishes and welfare
- the likelihood of court proceedings (criminal and civil)
- the age and development of the child
- the degree of expediency required.

The preliminary interview and planning are intended to provide an opportunity to establish whether video recording is appropriate. These arrangements were agreed in Leicestershire from the outset and have remained unchanged, following a recent review of practice. However, there have been some teething problems with implementing them which will be explored later in this chapter.

Resource implications

The practicalities of establishing an adequate number of video suites in appropriate locations involved a great deal of negotiation. It was possible only to make a rough estimate of the number of interviews that were likely to be recorded. The principle issue was not the sheer number of interviews but the undesirability of transporting distressed children long distances across a large county. There was also concern about identifying suitable premises and, as ever, finding the money to convert and equip them. In the event, four sites were established which proved more than adequate to ensure that a video suite is available when required, but they are less than ideally placed geographically, particularly for access from the City of Leicester where the greatest number of child protection cases originate. Cost has been another significant factor, the conversion and equipping of the social services facility alone having totalled in the region of £35,000.

Training

A programme of joint training was established for police officers and social workers. For reasons of operational expediency this was pared down from a proposed ten days to five. A key issue for social services in preparing for implementation of the *Memorandum* was the number of staff to be trained. The majority of child protection referrals are handled by the social services access teams which operate generically across all client groups. The possibility of establishing specialist investigative teams, along the lines advocated by the Cleveland Report (DHSS, 1988) was discounted at an early stage as running counter to the generic ethos of the access system. This issue has remained a contentious one, with some other local authorities having decided that this was the best, and perhaps the only, way to pursue effective joint work under the new arrangements.

Operational managers were keen to ensure that there were adequate numbers of social workers trained to guarantee that one was available when required. Set against this were the costs of training large numbers; concern that workers would quickly lose skills because they were doing so few interviews; the difficulty in establishing close working relationships between police and large numbers of social workers, and the practical difficulties in planning joint training with widely differing numbers between the two professional groups. In the event, about 70 social workers were trained in a programme of courses run over six months. A survey carried out in 1995 confirmed that many of these trained social workers have carried out few if any interviews. However, turnover of staff has resulted in a shortage of trained workers in particular locations and necessitated further training to replace them.

Implementing the *Memorandum*

The experience of implementing the *Memorandum* in Leicestershire has been mixed. Some of the initial fears of social workers have been allayed but a more subtle pattern of unease at the impact of the new arrangements on social work practice can be discerned. The number of interviews conducted has been high but, as Table 2.1 shows, the number actually used in criminal proceedings is small.

Table 2.1   Video recorded interviews conducted in Leicestershire in 1994 and 1995

	1994	1995
Joint investigations resulting in video recording of evidence	350	345
Number of video recordings submitted to the CPS	139	78*
Number of video recordings used in Crown Court proceedings	10*	10*

(* These figures are approximate as exact numbers were not available)

These figures need to be treated with some caution but a rather startling pattern emerges. In 1994, for example, only 40 per cent of the video recordings made were submitted to the Crown Prosecution Service (CPS) and less than 3 per cent of the total went on to be used in criminal proceedings. Of course this does not take account of guilty pleas which may have been prompted by the presence of a video recording and which are unquantified. It is also possible that the availability of video evidence makes the CPS more likely to take proceedings but Davies et al. (1995) suggest that there is little evidence available to support this idea. The fact that only between a quarter and half of the recordings made find their way to the CPS suggests in itself that the criteria established in Leicestershire for deciding when to conduct a video recorded interview are not working as intended.

The role of the social worker

Some of the concerns about the effect of the new arrangements on the role of social workers appear to have been borne out in practice. The requirements of evidential interviewing, combined with greater experience of the group of specialist police officers who are conducting the majority of interviews, means that social workers rarely take the lead. Social workers report that they are often relegated to the role of observers and technicians, operating the equipment and making notes for the interview log. One experienced social worker said:

> we usually agree that the police officer should take the lead but unless there is a third person there someone has to look after the equipment to make sure it is running properly. This means sitting in the observation room. I don't feel that I have the expertise to do anything if the machine does go wrong and it seems like a waste of a social worker's time just sitting there taking notes.

This appears to confirm the view of Wattam (1992) and others that the role of the social worker in representing the child's broader welfare also takes a back seat. The picture is not entirely consistent, however, as one or two social workers in the department report taking the lead in the majority of interviews. These are social workers involved in relatively large numbers of interviews who may be particularly confident and assertive, but it does demonstrate that they need not necessarily be relegated to a secondary role.

Perhaps as a result of this disparity in roles, combined with a pragmatic view taken by many police officers that video recording is the best way to record an interview, the police were perceived by social workers from the outset as being more ready and willing to make recorded interviews. Social workers and team managers reported that they felt unsure of their ground in discussing whether video recording was appropriate in particular situations. There were a number of reasons given for this reluctance to assume that video recording was always the best way forward. The initial lack of confidence in front of the camera and unfamiliarity with the equipment has already been referred to. In addition, there was concern about moving children across the county; about the impact on children of being video recorded; and about the extent of the time and resources being committed, with apparently little end result in the way of videos being used in court. There were also fears, subsequently confirmed by Davies et al. (1995) that the availability of video recordings would give defence lawyers more opportunity to discredit the way in which evidence was obtained, and that police officers and social workers giving evidence would come under fierce attack about the conduct of the interview. Underlying these more concrete concerns were increasing doubts about their own role in a process increasingly being taken over by the requirements of the criminal justice system.

The *Memorandum* in practice

If the spirit and wording of the Leicestershire joint protocol can be considered broadly satisfactory, putting it into practice proved to be more problematic. In particular, there were difficulties in ensuring adequate communication and planning. Operational circumstances sometimes made it difficult to ensure that a trained social worker and police officer were available at a suitable time. Usually these situations were negotiated and a compromise solution was reached. At other times social workers reported that the police had apparently decided, in advance of any discussion or initial assessment of the situation, that a video interview was necessary and had booked one of the video suites. Occasionally, these situations led to the police conducting an interview without a social worker being present. This is not to suggest that the responsibility for such problems can all be laid at the door of the police; there was undoubtedly a shared responsibility for difficulties in communication. Relationships between the two agencies have been good and there was a genuine will on the part of each to work together and to achieve high standards of practice. However, it is indicative of the sort of problems that can arise at the early stages of the investigation and which can both complicate the decision whether or not to video and impede effective planning. Certainly the pre-interview assessment of whether a child has something of substance to say, and which is referred to in the Leicestershire protocol, was often omitted. A review of joint working arrangements in 1995 concluded that the protocol was satisfactory but that more care was needed in implementing it. In particular, it was seen as essential that each situation should be approached with an open mind and for a genuinely joint decision to be taken about whether to conduct a video recorded interview. The constraints on the time of social workers and police officers was, however, recognised as a significant obstacle to achieving consistent best practice.

The role of the Crown Prosecution Service (CPS)

One of the initial expectations was that the existence of a video recording of the interview, as evidence-in-chief in a criminal trial, would make it easier to ensure that the child received therapy without risking accusations of contaminating evidence. Sadly this has often proved not to be the case. The Department of Health Study (1994) reports that half of the local authorities surveyed thought that it was actually more difficult to combine treatment with the gathering of evidence than before the implementation of the *Memorandum*.

The perception is that the Crown Prosecution Service has often resisted efforts to secure therapy for children pre-trial. At a national level the CPS has maintained, correctly, that while they would like the police and CPS to be consulted about referral of a child for therapy, the decision is not theirs. This national position has not always been borne out by local experience. Historically in Leicestershire there have been difficulties in the lines of communication between the three agencies about such decisions, with a more distant relationship between the CPS and social services than exists in some other areas. Social workers experienced a reluctance by the CPS to sanction therapy and there were instances of very distressed children being unable to receive the help they needed. Fortunately, this situation greatly improved after changes in the approach of the CPS and the development of a jointly agreed policy on pre-trial therapy.

The effect on police/social services relations

It is not easy to assess the overall impact of the *Memorandum* on the relationship between the police and social services departments. This is in part because the picture varies from one area to the next but also because the effects are complex. One of the key aims of the guidance was to improve communication and mutual understanding of the respective roles of the two agencies (Wattam, 1992). Taking a narrow focus on the joint approach to investigative interviewing in pursuit of criminal investigation the effects may appear positive. There is evidence of a gradual improvement in interviewing techniques and the development of positive working relationships between some police officers and social workers. We would suggest, however, that this is achieved at a considerable cost and that the longer term effect may well be to place a great strain on inter-agency relationships as the statutory responsibility of social services to safeguard the child's interests is compromised.

This tension has been reflected at a national level in the public debate between the Association of Chief Police Officers and the Association of Directors of Social Services which followed the publication of the research papers by the Department of Health and the Home Office. This debate reflected the different perspectives of the two agencies. The police representative was broadly in favour of the changes brought about by the *Memorandum* (see Chapter 3). The social services view (represented by Brian Waller, one of the authors of this chapter) was more cautious, expressing doubts about the benefits to children of the new arrangements (Waller, 1995).

The research picture

We would argue that the two principal documents evaluating the implementation of the *Memorandum* reflect the differing agency views we have described above. It is interesting that the Home Office (Davies et al., 1995) and the Department of Health (1994) appear to have embarked on their separate research projects with little communication or co-operation. *The Child, the Court and the Video* (Department of Health, 1994), published a few months in advance of the Home Office report (1995), is based largely upon a survey of social services departments and reflects their mostly critical view of the new arrangements. Some of these criticisms are based upon the court process and its damaging effects on children but many respondents felt that the *Memorandum* itself fails children. One authority summed up its views thus: '(a) the needs of criminal proceedings dominate; (b) the process does not encourage child-focused work and (c) given such usage of the video tapes produced, is it worth the experience?' (Department of Health, 1994: 53).

The Home Office sponsored research (Davies et al., 1995) includes an evaluation of video tapes and information about criminal court process and outcomes as well as a postal survey of professionals' views. This study confirms the concerns expressed by social workers, including their feelings of being 'de-skilled and divorced from the investigative process' (Davies et al., 1995: 8) but is rather more encouraging about the impact of the *Memorandum*. This more positive approach may reflect the focus of the research on the interview process itself and it is pleasing to hear that the majority of video tapes viewed by the researchers conform to the main requirements of the *Memorandum* and demonstrate a general level of good practice. The report concludes that the *Memorandum* has resulted in an increase in the interview skills of social workers and hence, in some ways, improved the service. The report also suggests that an increasing number of children are gaining access to the courts. The effect on children is reported as being mixed, some of them valuing a sense of being taken seriously through having their interview video recorded and others feeling let down when the 'stressful experience of providing evidence leads to no further action'.

The Home Office report acknowledges that only a tiny minority of video recordings reach court and the apparent waste of resources involved in recording so many, with a suggestion that 'some form of pre-interview screening could lead to significant savings in material and human resources'. What the report understandably does not address is the rather more nebulous subject of the child's general welfare and the extent to which the impact of the *Memorandum* on social workers is reducing their capacity to represent this.

The dilemma for social services

In recent years an increasing proportion of the resources of social services departments and other agencies has been committed to the process of investigating, conferencing and supervising cases of suspected child abuse, often to the detriment of other child care work. Reports from the Social Services Inspectorate (Department of Health, 1995) and the Audit Commission (1994) suggest that local authorities are failing in their responsibilities under Section 17 of the Children Act to provide services to children in need, including preventative services to children who may be at future risk. The research commissioned by the Department of Health also suggests that the child protection system, while operating effectively in the most serious cases, draws in a large number of families inappropriately. It is suggested that the effect upon these families is very negative and they are rarely offered alternative services if no child protection concerns are identified. Social services departments are being urged to re-examine their approach to child protection work and to place the emphasis on Section 47 'enquiries' (the term used in the Children Act) rather than investigations. This is not just a matter of semantics but embodies the notion that we assess the needs of children in the round, not merely their need for immediate protection.

This is not to suggest that suspicions or allegations of sexual abuse, which prompt the majority of video recorded interviews, should be taken other than very seriously and be subject to thorough investigation. Rather, it is the increasing emphasis on the interests of the criminal justice system in the course of the investigation which causes us concern. The requirements of the *Memorandum* have been criticised by the police and social workers as being too rigid and inflexible; for example, in the expectation that a child will be able to tell his or her story in a single interview lasting one hour. As confidence has grown with experience, many interviewers have become more relaxed and are able to use the *Memorandum* as guidance rather than following it to the letter. However, the standard of proof in criminal cases is higher than that allowed in civil proceedings and the desire of interviewers, particularly police officers, not to risk having a tape ruled as inadmissible means that they may avoid some avenues of enquiry; for example, asking leading questions of a younger child or one who is finding it difficult to talk. The answers to such questions may not be admissible in criminal proceedings but could provide information which is essential to protect a child in care proceedings. A senior solicitor in Leicestershire expressed her view that these issues have had a negative effect on the local authority's ability to establish a case in some circumstances.

It is almost certainly the case that the development of specialist investigative teams within social services departments would improve the general quality of social work input to video recorded interviews and enable social workers to operate on a more equal footing with their police colleagues. But this emphasises the dilemma for social services. To follow this path would confirm social workers in the investigative role which they have increasingly assumed in recent years. However, the separation of the investigative function from the pursuit of the broader welfare needs of the child may well be counter-productive and lead to the ever greater predominance of the former over the latter.

Conclusions

For many children, the conviction of an adult who has sexually abused them helps their recovery and is in the interests of justice. It may also help to protect them and other children. The introduction of the *Memorandum of Good Practice* has improved interview techniques and the skills of those who conduct them. These are positive benefits and should be welcomed. However, there are some worrying implications of the new arrangements which we have identified. The effects upon the nature of the social work role are extensive and coincide with a time when social services departments are being urged to re-examine their approach to child protection. Some commentators have gone so far as to suggest that social services should withdraw from the investigative role altogether and leave it to the police or to a specialist agency such as the NSPCC (Parton, 1995).

The evaluations of practice under the *Memorandum* (Department of Health, 1994; Davies et al., 1995) confirm that very few of the thousands of videos made each year are ever used in court proceedings. This suggests that we have created a system which is wasteful both of time and resources. The benefits to children are uncertain and the failure to implement the full recommendations of the Pigot Report means that children are still subjected to the ordeal of hostile cross examination in an open courtroom.

However, it is probably safe to assume that the *Memorandum* is here to stay. It has been generally accepted and within the criminal justice system its benefits are seen to outweigh any disadvantages. Some of the problems we have identified are complex in nature and not easily addressed. What, then, can be done?

First, there needs to be further national debate about the role of social workers in *Memorandum* investigations and interviews. Specialist teams may be an answer, but their establishment will serve to further reinforce the separation of child protection from child welfare.

Secondly, the recommendations of the Pigot Report should be fully implemented, allowing cross-examination of children to take place before the trial proper begins, thus sparing children the ordeal of appearing in court.

Thirdly, the *Memorandum* should be revised, to include clearer guidance on the decision to video record, with a view to reducing the number of interviews conducted. Formal provision should be made for a pre-interview assessment to establish whether the child has something to say, whether a video interview is appropriate and to allow for better planning of the interview based upon the child's age and development.

Finally, the arrangements for training of social workers and police officers should be strengthened and consideration given to a national scheme for accreditation of interviewers.

These proposals are drawn from our experiences in Leicestershire, which appear to closely reflect those reported nationally. We believe that if implemented they would address many of the concerns reported by social workers and enhance inter-agency cooperation. More importantly, they would improve the service to children, reduce the inevitable stress of the investigation, and improve our ability to meet the full range of their needs.

References

Audit Commission (1994), *Seen But Not Heard*, London: HMSO.

Davies, G., Wilson, C., Mitchell, R. and Milsom, J. (1995), *Videotaping Children's Evidence: An Evaluation*, London: Home Office.

Department of Health, Social Services Inspectorate (1995), *Child Protection: Messages From Research*, London: HMSO.

Department of Health, Social Services Inspectorate (1994), *The Child, The Court and The Video*, Heywood, Lancs: Health Publications Unit.

Department of Health and Social Security (DHSS) (1988), *Report of the Inquiry into Child Abuse in Cleveland*, London: HMSO.

Home Office (1989) *Report of the Advisory Group on Video Evidence*, Chairman Judge Thomas Pigot QC, London: Home Office.

Home Office and Department of Health (1992), *Memorandum of Good Practice*, London: HMSO.

Leicestershire Constabulary and Leicestershire Social Services Department (1993), *Joint Agency Procedures on Video Recording Interviews with Children*, Leicester: Leicestershire Constabulary.

Parton, N. (1995), Presentation to a Conference at Lancaster University, January.

Waller B. (1995), 'Sex abuse: the hidden trial of child victims', *Guardian*, 25 January 1995.

Wattam, C. (1992), *Making a Case in Child Protection*, Harlow, Essex: Longman.

3 The *Memorandum*: the police view

Tony Butler

The overriding objective implicit in the introduction of the video recording of child witness evidence must be concerned with the achievement of justice for children. Consequently, a review of the use of video recording must attempt to determine if it has increased the chances that children will receive justice through the courts. This simple question masks the complex debate which has surrounded the experience of the use of video recordings in the investigation and prosecution of allegations of abuse against children. Furthermore, the extent to which children have benefited from the changes to the law extends far beyond the consideration of the role of the *Memorandum of Good Practice on Video Recorded Interviews with Child Witnesses for Criminal Proceedings* (Home Office, 1992).

These comments on the police perspective will range beyond the limited framework set out in the *Memorandum,* because it is an illusion to assume that merely changing a document will change the behaviour of individuals and institutions responsible for providing children with justice. The term 'justice' includes the achievement of protection for vulnerable children without the necessity for invoking the provisions of the criminal justice system. It should not be assumed that police officers working with children are motivated by a narrow perspective of seeking criminal convictions of alleged perpetrators. They share with other members of caring agencies a commitment to the protection of children but, as the Foreword to the *Memorandum* points out, 'the interests of justice and the interests of the child are not alternatives'.

Child protection should not be seen on a continuum from policing at one end to caring at the other. In reality, policing and caring are aims which run in parallel. There is no doubt that the impact of *Working Together* (Department of Health, 1991) and professional experience has created a greater sense of shared working and professional cooperation. But it is also important to ensure some differentiation of those professional perspectives. It is likely that the police service will always remain essentially an investigative agency, with welfare being the principle remit of social workers. There is nothing divisive in such an approach as the strength of a team is drawn from the different skills of the players.

In the process of taking stock of current practice and effectiveness, professional diversity should be seen as a strength and not a weakness. However, it does raise questions about clarifying the goals of the services provided to children at risk and in need. There can be a tendency for the goals to become clouded and the debate to be focused on the means. For example, the fact that children may be traumatised by a court appearance does not, in itself, mean that cases should never go to court or alleged perpetrators should not have an appropriate opportunity to defend themselves. The goal must be for both the child victim and the alleged perpetrator to receive justice. The challenge is to determine how those goals can be achieved.

The research

During 1995, a number of significant research projects was published. The three major contributions were by Professor Graham Davies (Davies et al., 1995), Joan Holton of the Department of Health (Social Services Inspectorate, 1994), and the collation of papers *Child Protection: Messages from Research* (Department of Health, 1995). It is important, however, to recognise the limitations of research and not to read into it facts which cannot be supported. Probably one of the most significant limitations in the current research is evidence about the impact on child victims of the investigation and the criminal justice process. It is not surprising that children and their carers are reluctant to continue their involvement with research projects after the end of a trial and, therefore, the opportunity to receive detailed information about their experience and perceptions of that experience are difficult to obtain. Where information is available, for example, the work by Sharland et al., (1995), it suggests that children do value justice through formal processes. Furthermore, where alleged perpetrators are not prosecuted or are acquitted, children feel let down by the system. Consequently, the value of the criminal justice process in its contribution to healing the trauma caused by abuse should not be overlooked.

The overwhelming message from the research is one of complexity, dealing with uncertainty and facing almost on every occasion a unique set of circumstances which requires a unique response. It is attempting to create some form of order out of this complexity which is the challenge for policy makers, in this context there are four points which are worthy of specific comment.

The research is helpful in reminding practitioners of the broader context in which their services are set. The question what is normal or abnormal behaviour in family relationships is a useful starting point to consider potential actions. The research demonstrates the difficulty of determining when there should be interventions by caring agencies in respect of physical and emotional abuse but it is probably more clear cut in relation to alleged sexual abuse. Although the majority of cases involving children in sexual abuse are related to family members or close relatives and friends, the research does suggest that a clear distinction may be made as to what is normal and abnormal behaviour. Consequently, there does appear to be a need to respond to sexual abuse as qualitatively different to other potential sources of harm to children.

Following on from the first point, the research does provide support to the notion that sexual abuse by its very nature is a particularly harmful and emotionally damaging event. Furthermore, while a single event of physical harm may be overlooked, a single event of sexual abuse could have a substantial and long-lasting impact on the child victim.

What does the research tell us about the work of police officers and social workers? To answer this question, it is worth looking at Davies et al. (1995), the report prepared by Social Services Inspectorate (Department of Health, 1994) and an older but nevertheless relevant research project conducted by NCH Action for Children (Prior et al. 1994). The evidence from these three pieces of work support the observation that police officers and social workers have made great efforts to improve their services to children and, perhaps above all others in the system, have changed and developed into a more coherent and professional service. To some extent, the recognition by these practitioners that others in the system have not achieved similar improvements is a significant source of frustration and stress. In fact, it is not an exaggeration to say that when making a decision to proceed with a case following investigation, the likely damage that the court hearing will do to a child is a factor which practitioners have to take into account. In fact, justice may be denied the child in his or her own interests because the process of achieving justice is perceived as likely to be too harmful.

The difficulties experienced by practitioners in determining how they should proceed in cases where there is a suspicion of abuse raises direct legal questions which reflect the different responsibilities set out in Section 17 and Section 47 of the Children Act 1989. The purpose of Section 17, to develop a service plan for children in need or at risk falls short of the investigative approach characterised by Section 47. Unfortunately, it is difficult to determine how to tailor services for a child without undertaking some form of fact finding which looks very much like an investigation. This dilemma may be less in cases of suspected child sexual abuse because, as the research points out, the risks and the inherent potential harm to children appear to be qualitatively different to other forms of abuse or risk. Consequently, it is likely that the investigation route will be the chosen approach. However, such a choice should be undertaken and pursued in a way that, at each stage, the needs of the child are reconsidered. It would be a great error to assume that all investigations referred to the police involve every part of the process; in fact, many do not involve an interview with the child and, furthermore, many further allegations do not progress in investigation terms beyond an initial interview.

The *Memorandum* – some views from police officers

Police officers working in the field of child abuse investigations have found the framework of the *Memorandum* and the specific guidance it contains a useful contribution to improving their skills and their effectiveness. The major benefit has been to provide, probably for the first time, a formal framework within which interviewing of children can take place. Police officers were obliged to recognise the variation in emotional and conceptual development of children and in the light of this recognition, design their interview techniques in response. In conversations with officers, they openly discuss the shortcomings that they can now identify from earlier interviewing styles which preceded the introduction of the *Memorandum*. There have also been changes to the environment in which children were interviewed. Prior to its introduction, it was not unusual for children to be interviewed together and, furthermore, where they were in care, it was not uncommon for them to be interviewed at the children's home.

The *Memorandum* has been a major catalyst for change. It has brought police officers and social workers closer together, thus leading to more understanding of each other's roles and also enabling skills and experience to be exchanged. However, there are some distinct variations in the practice of collaboration. In some areas social workers will not become involved in cases where the alleged abuser is outside the family. This can lead to a significant proportion of cases, up to 40 per cent, where there is no formal involvement of social workers in the investigation of the case. There are also differences in the working methods of social work departments. In some areas, social workers specialise in child abuse cases, but in others they are more generalist. One important consequence of the generalist approach is the lower level of expertise and experience the social workers achieve. This is a particularly relevant point when the decision about who should lead an interview is taken.

In the light of experience, there are some points of interpretation in the *Memorandum* which could usefully be reconsidered. The decision as to when to video record the interview has become somewhat contentious. There has been a significant improvement in the system of planning interviews, with much greater emphasis on collating and evaluating information prior to the decision to interview. However, as later discussions will highlight, this is a complex area, where competing demands are difficult to resolve. The guidance on second interviews in paragraph 1.11 of the *Memorandum* is also seen as too restrictive in the light of experience. This point is linked to the advice about the length of the interview not exceeding an hour (Home Office, 1992: para. 2.17).

Issues from a police perspective – the decision to interview

The *Memorandum* has improved the clarity of the issues to be considered in the early stages of an investigation and has emphasised the need for careful and systematic planning for interviews. But the decision to undertake a video recorded interview remains the role of the investigator based on professional judgement using the facts available at the time. There has been much debate about this issue with the clear implication that the police are making too many videos.

Unfortunately, some of the criticisms made of the decision to interview are based on comparing the number of video tapes produced and the number of cases reaching court in which video recorded evidence is used. These figures have to be treated with a high degree of caution. For example, the early figures were not reliably comparable because they failed to take into account the developing use of the technique. The only reliable means of making these comparisons is over an extended period, probably at least 18 months to two years to track an individual investigation. The second point which must be considered is to take account of those cases where a plea of guilty is entered. Finally, unless there are documented reasons to establish why the video was not played, it may have as much to do with the individual idiosyncrasies of the judge, counsel or the quality of the court playback equipment, as a failure by the police interviewer.

Any attempt to measure the effectiveness of video recording by comparing the numbers of interviews carried out now with those carried out prior to the implementation of the *Memorandum*, is doomed to failure because no records were kept by the police or the Lord Chancellor's Department prior to the implementation. It is quite possible that the improved planning and the provisions of the *Memorandum* have in fact reduced the number of interviews.

By the very nature of the offences being investigated, any interview is likely to be a stressful experience. There is no evidence to suggest that the process of video recording is any more stressful than any other procedure that currently exists; certainly it is the best all-round alternative that has been devised to serve the interests of the child and the criminal justice system.

Research has not indicated that video recording is an inefficient or wasteful method of gathering evidence. In practice, the video interview may enable other child care professionals to hear the child's account at first hand rather than have to subject the child to a further interview.

If there is to be a substantial reduction in the number of video recorded interviews carried out, will this mean that children making allegations of abuse are not to be interviewed or given an opportunity to relate their experience? Plainly this situation would be unacceptable. Assuming therefore that some children, while not being video recorded would still have to be interviewed, it is incumbent of the people demanding a reduction in the number of video interviews to explain how that interview is to be documented or recorded. There are only two other alternative methods, note taking by hand and audio tape. The first method is notoriously inaccurate, long-winded and will be the subject of challenge at a later date. The second method, in terms of cost, has little significant benefit but fails to record important evidence about the child's demeanour and body language.

The problems caused by the failure to properly record interviews, even at very early stages in an investigation, have been graphically illustrated in the High Court of Justice Family Division. His Honour Mr Justice Connell was hearing the case which became known as the South Pembrokeshire Paedophile Cases. In his judgment he said:

> Of course there are situations where it is not possible to video what a child says; for instance when the child speaks on the spur of the moment. In this case Dyfed were operating a policy at the relevant times that a child would not be video recorded on first encounter with a social worker, and then not until there was reason to believe that the child had something relevant that he or she wanted to say. As it happens a number of the crucial allegations in this case were made by children at such a first encounter which was usually shortly after the child had been removed from home. Consequently none of these was videoed and a very large amount of time has been spent in court on testing the recollections and notes of those who were present when the allegation was made. I understand the thinking behind Dyfed's policy, but the result is that I am left in significant doubt as to the extent to which I can place reliance upon these allegations. In short, a direct consequence of this policy has been significantly to weaken a number of the cases of the Local Authority and it is as well that those who imposed it should realise this.

While there may be some scope to reduce the number of interviews currently taking place, this will require careful thought and consideration. On balance, it is probably preferable to interview a child to be reassured that there is no cause for concern rather than to fail to interview and thereby deny the child either the protection or the justice that he or she is entitled to receive.

Issues from a police perspective – training

The research carried out by Davies et al. (1995) acknowledges that skills have been developed by police officers and social workers in the interviewing of child witnesses and victims. However, experience is raising two issues, first the quality of the training and second, the opportunities for some social workers to build expertise based on practice.

Research by the Department of Health commented,

> Courses varied in length. One was a ten-day specialist course on video interviewing and in another area a two-day video course was attached to a five-day basic joint child protection investigation course. Thus the time available to practice video interviewing skills varied widely, as did course content. Some courses concentrated on working with children and how to communicate with them, others on legal issues, some studied the memory and the psychology of a child in an interviewing situation. Training courses in two authorities employed actors to take the part of children in simulated interviews on video. This method was seen by both trainers and trainees as a very successful way of learning new skills (Department of Health, 1994).

One approach could be the development of a nationally recognised system of accreditation for training courses and standards achieved by police officers and social workers. Nobody would dispute that the interviewing of children requires specialist skills; within the police service the expertise of firearms officers, dog handlers, scenes of crime officers is recognised, not only because of the job they carry out but because there is a recognisable recruitment process, a training course, a standard to be achieved and then subsequently maintained. Recognition of skills will substantially reduce the feeling of marginalisation that many child protection officers currently experience.

The practice of some social services departments of using a generalist approach to child abuse investigation and as a consequence training larger numbers of staff, may devalue the contribution that social workers are able to make on training courses because their staff do not have the depth of experience which is only attainable from working in specialised units. This may later lead to concerns about their confidence and ability so that it becomes inevitable that the police will tend to lead when interviewing children. An accredited form of training would demonstrate an ability to undertake interviews to an approved standard.

Issues from a police perspective – welfare of the child

The video recording of child witness evidence was introduced to reduce the stress and trauma. There may be a debate about the extent to which this has been achieved at the investigation stage, but there is no argument that during the period before the trial and at trial, very little has changed to reduce the stress of the process. One of the principle sources of anxiety is the uncertainty about the trial process.

Last minute changes and the unwillingness of some judges to make decisions in cases which one of their colleagues will hear, results in frustration for those involved in the case, an inability to properly prepare a witness and, ultimately, unnecessary trauma being experienced by a child witness. The Royal Commission on Criminal Justice recommended that a judge should have powers to make a binding ruling on any question as to the admissibility of evidence and on any other question of law relating to the case. If pre-trial hearings are to be made more effective, then incentives and sanctions should be put in place to encourage counsel to achieve a proper balance between preparatory work and advocacy at the trial itself.

The Criminal Procedure and Investigation Act 1996 may resolve this issue with the introduction of binding decisions at pre-trial hearings thereby creating more certainty about the arrangements for trial. It will be essential to ensure that the decision of the judge can only be reopened if new information comes to light before the trial.

An important contribution to the reduction in the pre-trial stress can be made by assigning an independent adult to look after the child's interests. Unfortunately the provision of a supporter for the child is not without its problems. *The Child Witness Pack* (NSPCC/ChildLine, 1993) was introduced without identifying who was to perform the role and how it was going to be funded. This has led to the introduction of some *ad hoc* arrangements and to many children not receiving any preparation for court (Davies et al., 1995). For example, police officers have often been left to assume the responsibilities. Where there has been a willingness for other statutory or voluntary agencies to take on the work, there have been difficulties with funding. Finally, the system can fail at the last moment because judges have been refusing to allow the independent adult to accompany the child into the video room at court. The ruling by Deputy Chief Justice Tasker-Watkins in October 1991 (Practice Direction), has led to other judges refusing to allow the child to be accompanied by anyone other than the court usher. Although the usher may be trained, this overlooks the need for these traumatised children to have the support of a trusted and familiar adult. In one recent case an application was made for the boy to be accompanied by the independent adult and it was also pointed out to the judge that he would not talk about his experience in front of a woman. The application was refused, the female usher accompanied the boy into the interview room and he said nothing. The case was dismissed.

Issues from a police perspective – conduct of the trial

There is an increasing feeling among practitioners that the officers and social workers who conduct the interviews are also on trial at the crown court. They are often subjected to detailed and hostile questioning about their actions prior to and during the interview of the child. A developing trend by defence counsel is to discredit the process of obtaining the evidence from the child. This is reflected in the observation by the judge in the Dyfed case. The extent of this approach was seen in a crown court case where the judge was pressed by defence counsel to rule the video evidence inadmissible on the basis that the strict interpretation of the *Memorandum* had not been followed. Neither counsel or the judge implied any bad faith on the part of any person involved in interviewing the child witnesses. Defence counsel submitted that the child's video recorded evidence should be excluded under Section 78 of the Police and Criminal Evidence Act 1984, and the trial judge agreed.

This case may be unusual, but it does illustrate a worrying trend where the extreme application of the due process model is making the opportunity for children to receive justice more and more difficult. The decision also seems to fly in the face of the intention of the working group which produced the *Memorandum*. The introduction to the *Memorandum* contains the following statement.

> A video recording that does not strictly comply with the Memorandum will not automatically be ruled admissible. On the contrary, it was Parliament's clear intention that such video recordings of children's testimony should be admitted unless, in the opinion of the Judge, it would clearly be contrary to the interests of justice to do so (Home Office, 1992: 1).

Although there have been some improvements in the treatment of children in the trial since the introduction of video recorded evidence in 1992 (Butler, 1993), there is a long way to go before the interests of the child witness are recognised in practice. The full Pigot recommendations extend video recording to the defence cross-examination of the child (Home Office, 1989). If implemented this would reduce the uncertainty of a long wait for the trial to take place and would mean that the child would not have to undergo the ordeal of attending court. However, even if implemented it may not achieve the laudable aims of the Pigot recommendations. The issues are more concerned with the nature of the approach taken by defence counsel and the difficult task of the judge to control the worst excesses of the adversarial system.

The *Memorandum* places great stress on the need for police officers to understand the complexities of child language development and their cognitive capacities in relation to time and memory. These are critical skills in the context of investigative interviewing. Observations of the court process show little evidence of the capacity of counsel and judges to have the same high degree of understanding. Consequently the conduct of the case and the evidential value of the child's evidence is substantially impaired. These same lawyers would not dream of hearing evidence from an adult who did not fully understand English without an interpreter, but it does not seem to cross their minds that complex sentence construction, the use of double negatives and a range of other techniques may be substantially disadvantageous to the child witness. The observation of the trials in the Home Office research (Davies et al.,1995), showed that 86 per cent of the questions the child witnesses were asked by the prosecution were 'mainly central information', whereas, in the case of cross-examination by the defence 46 per cent of the questions were 'mainly peripheral information' and 4 per cent were 'mainly irrelevancies'.

There is no question that people accused of child abuse face some of the most serious criminal charges and children share the same capacity as adults to tell lies. These realities should not, however, be used as an excuse to intimidate, confuse and traumatise child witnesses. There are professional and robust methods of challenging children's evidence without resorting to these tactics. There is a suspicion that the worst excesses of the defence may be a symptom of poor training in child development processes and inadequate preparation for the case by counsel who may have only received the brief when he or she arrived at court on the morning of the trial.

Future prospects

There is no doubt that children who have been the victims of physical or sexual abuse receive a better response from police officers and social workers as a result of the guidelines in the *Memorandum*. There are also opportunities to further improve that response. The source of those improvements, however, is more likely to be achieved by professionals developing the state of their knowledge and skills rather than a rewriting of the *Memorandum*. There are some limitations to the *Memorandum* in the context of general work with children and as Bentovim et al. (1995) discuss, particular problems of interviewing highly traumatised children and those with learning disabilities. But one of the most important determinants of the quality of the interview is the experience and skill of the interviewer (Wiseman et al., 1992).

Despite current problems it is important to remain optimistic about the future. It should not be impossible for children to be given greater protection from abuse and for them to achieve justice in the courts. Three key points summarise issues which would make significant contributions to the future improvements:

- The development of national standards of training leading to formal accreditation. This would create further opportunities for professional collaboration between police officers and social workers. It would also help to reduce the opportunities for defence counsel to discredit the evidence of the children even before it is heard.
- The provision of a national system of independent adults to support child witnesses would bring a proper recognition to the critical role of these workers to the reduction of stress for the child witness. It would also have to address the issue of funding, training and a reappraisal of the judicial direction to exclude them from the video room when the child is giving evidence.
- If there is to be a major review of the *Memorandum*, then it should include guidance to judges and counsel on the treatment of children in court. In addition, there should be a requirement for more training for judges and counsel who deal with child witnesses cases to ensure they have a working knowledge of issues such as child language and memory development.

These three points will not solve all the problems overnight, but as experience has shown, progress can be made through goodwill and a willingness to change. It is also important to retain a commitment to the principle defined in the foreword to the *Memorandum* that 'the interests of justice and the interests of the child are not alternatives'. This principle may still be somewhat illusive, but that does not mean we should stop trying.

Acknowledgement

The author wishes to acknowledge the contribution made to the preparation of this chapter by Ian Clark, Karen Cotterill, Sally Miller and Miriam Beard.

References

Bentovim, A., Bentovim, M., Vizard, E. and Wiseman, M., (1995), 'Facilitating interviews with children who may have been sexually abused', *Child Abuse Review*, 4, 246–62.

Butler, A.J.P. (1993), 'Spare the child', *Police Review*, 10 December 1993.

Davies, G., Wilson, C., Mitchell, R. and Milsom, J., (1995), *Videotaping Children's Evidence: An Evaluation*, London: Home Office.

Department of Health (1995), *Child Protection: Messages from Research*, London: HMSO.

Department of Health (1991), *Working Together*, London: HMSO.

Home Office and Department of Health (1992) *Memorandum of Good Practice on Video Recorded Interviews with Child Witnesses for Criminal Proceedings,* London: HMSO.

Home Office (1989), *Report of the Advisory Group on Video Evidence,* Chairman Judge Thomas Pigot QC, London: Home Office.

NSPCC/ChildLine (1993) *The Child Witness Pack,* London: NSPCC.

Prior, V., Lynch, M.A. and Glaser, D. (1994), *Messages from Children,* London: NCH Action for Children.

Sharland, E., Jones, D., Aldgate, J., Seal. H. and Croucher, M. (1995), 'Professional intervention in child sexual abuse', in Department of Health, *Child Protection: Messages From Research,* London: HMSO.

Department of Health, Social Services Inspectorate (1994), *The Child, The Court and The Video,* Heywood, Lancs: Health Publications Unit.

Wiseman, M., Vizard, E., Bentovim, A. and Leventhal, J. (1992), 'Reliability of videotaped interviews with children suspected of being sexually abused', *British Medical Journal,* 304, 1089–91.

4 The *Memorandum* and the guardian *ad litem*: whose rights, needs and interests?

Teresa O'Neill

This chapter will examine issues arising from the use of the *Memorandum of Good Practice in Video Recorded Interviews with Child Witnesses for Criminal Proceedings* (Home Office, 1992) to conduct interviews in child abuse investigations which result in the instigation of civil public law proceedings under the Children Act 1989, and the appointment of a guardian *ad litem*.

The chapter will consider the position and needs of children who are the subjects of investigations which result in criminal and/or civil proceedings. There are conflicts between the requirements of the criminal and civil courts and the principles of effective child centered investigations which enable children to speak about their experiences. The professionals involved in the investigation and the courts may contribute to the abuse and oppression of the child if they allow their own agendas and requirements to take precedence over the rights, needs and interests of the child.

The role and responsibilities of the guardian *ad litem* will be considered and a children's rights perspective which 'emphasises the importance of the child's own viewpoint and wishes [and sees] the child as a separate entity with rights to autonomy and freedom ... the subject rather than the object of others' actions and choices' (Fox Harding, 1991:155) will be adopted to argue that the guardian *ad litem* is in a unique position to empower the child, protect their rights and promote their wishes, views and interests, notwithstanding the inescapable tensions inherent in the role of the guardian *ad litem* as an officer of the court, mediator between the adult world of the courts and the child's world, and advocate ascertaining the wishes and feelings of the child.

Background

The recommendations of the Advisory Group on Video Evidence chaired by His Honour Judge Pigot (Home Office, 1989) suggested that 'a video recording prepared according to the standards recommended in this *Memorandum* is likely to be suitable for civil cases' on the basis that 'the rules of evidence which apply to civil proceedings are generally less stringent and so is the burden of proof' (Home Office, 1992: 4). It also suggested that video interviews should be made available in civil proceedings to minimise the number of occasions during the investigation that the child has to repeat their account of events. These recommendations were adopted and consequently, evidence presented to the court in civil, child protection proceedings is increasingly likely to include a video interview with the child: 'video interviews are now being introduced into civil proceedings as a matter of routine. All interviews have to be conducted as if they were for the Crown Court even though in civil proceedings a different standard of proof applies' (Holton, 1994: 50). These civil proceedings will be commenced under the provisions of the Children Act 1989 and will be concerned with whether the child has suffered or is likely to suffer significant harm and the level of protection which is needed. This will be determined on the basis of what is considered to be in the best interests of the child.

The Children Act 1989 enhanced the role of the guardian *ad litem* in civil, public law proceedings as the independent expert to act on behalf of the child who is the subject of the proceedings. S.41(2)(b) sets out the primary duty of the guardian to safeguard the interests of the child throughout the process of the investigation and the court proceedings. However, the need for the guardian to take account of other adult interests is recognised:

> The crucial importance of the guardian *ad litem*'s role is that it stands at the interface between the conflicting rights and powers of the courts, local authorities and natural and substitute parents in relation to the child. The guardian has to safeguard the child's interests ... to make a judgement between the potentially conflicting demands of children's rights, children's rescue, the autonomy of the family and the duty of the state (Department of Health 1992: 3).

The context

Attitudes to children and childhood are ambivalent and confused. The myth of a golden age of childhood held by adults, with its denial of realities such as child abuse and poverty, lead to children being alternately presented as 'monsters in our midst' with calls for changes in the law so that '10 year olds can be punished as if they were adults' (Moore, 1993: 11) and angels who are victims in need of protection from abuse. The idealisation of childhood means that child abuse is still regarded with outrage and incredulity with public opinion appearing to believe that such cases are 'aberrant, exceptional or quite rare' (Franklin, 1986: 3). The oscillation between children as angels and devils is dangerous and adds to the increasing moral panic and suspicion about children. The treatment of children within our social, political and legal systems reflects this ambivalence. Frost and Stein (1989) highlight their dilemma: 'they occupy a privileged space as the objects of our collective good intentions but simultaneously they are a large, oppressed minority without a voice and subject to a range of abuse and exploitation', echoing Franklin's (1986: 1,8) views that 'the term child has a connection less with chronology than with power' and that 'children form a large, long-suffering and oppressed grouping in society, a silent and unrepresented minority'.

Children are denied rights, often on the basis of what is paternalistically and subjectively deemed to be in their best interests. Franklin (1986: 18) describes paternalism as 'intervention in an individual's freedom of choice and/or action in an attempt to secure the best interests of that individual even though the individual may not recognise any advantage in such intervention, or indeed may perceive it to be injurious'. Any judgement about the best interests of a child must include their own wishes and views. Ensuring that the child is listened to and heard by those assessing their best interests presents the first dilemma. The second exists for the child who does not have a right to confidentiality and may be reluctant to speak. Newell (1988: 205) cautions that 'best interests is what one has to fall back on where there are no clear rights or where a child's extreme youth or disability prevent the exercise of rights that exist ... best interests are no substitute for rights'.

Children in our society suffer oppression, a concept described by McNay (1992: 50) as 'power relations' and defined thus: 'where relations are so structured that one person or group of people benefits at the expense of another person or group of people then the people who benefit can be said to have greater power in those relations'. Children will experience oppression along a number of dimensions which are interconnected, such as race, disability, class and economic status in addition to their age. It takes a number of forms such as material, emotional and ideological and occurs at an individual, familial and structural level. The child who is the subject of a child abuse investigation will have experienced their own powerlessness and lack of worth, frequently within 'trusted' relationships with parents or carers on whom they are emotionally dependent.

Professionals involved in the investigation of child abuse need to develop an understanding of oppression, how it affects the child they are interviewing and how their behaviour could be experienced as empowering or oppressive by the child. It is suggested that awareness of their own power and experience of oppression is essential if they are to use their power to empower rather than to dominate the child. Empowerment is described as 'the reduction of an overriding sense of powerlessness to direct one's own life ... a method by which helping professionals attempt to deal with power blocks experienced by negatively valued individuals' (Solomon 1987: 80).

O'Neill (1992: 38) reminds us that 'oppressors often try to suggest that they stand in a paternalistic relationship to those whom they oppress ... the vocabulary and trappings of paternalism are often misused to mask the unacceptable faces of power'. A power relationship framework described by Jones (1993) enables individuals to understand their own position in society and their capacity to be victimised or to dominate.

Summit (1983) identified the sexual abuse accommodation syndrome and pattern of behaviour that a child may adopt to cope with their abuse, the abuser and society. He illustrated how the accommodation syndrome reinforces the powerlessness of the child. Disclosure is not the normal behaviour, and retraction of the disclosure and 'accommodation' to the abuse may be an easier option for the child than dealing with the reactions and demands of professionals and community. Richardson and Bacon (1991) identify an equivalent 'professional accommodation syndrome' where a collusive silence may be maintained with a reluctance by professionals to be pro-active on behalf of children.

The guardian *ad litem* is an independent advocate, who must essentially be pro-active on behalf of the child, to empower the child so that they are able to express their wishes and feelings and to have them heard, to exercise choice and to facilitate their participation in decisions that are to be made on matters of concern to them. If the guardian is to do this unequivocally, they must develop an understanding of their own position within the power relationships of the patriarchal legal system and empower themselves to challenge practice which is not child-centred and which is likely to further oppress the child. The guardian must ensure that the child is visible in the proceedings, which requires that they first make themselves fully visible, in their role as an independent advocate for the child, as well as an officer of the court.

The investigation

Although the *Memorandum* is most frequently used in interviewing children who may have been sexually abused, it is also used in investigating other forms of abuse (Davies et al., 1995). The evidence of the child is regarded as central to the investigation, even where other evidence could be obtained (e.g. medical or from scene of crime), which places considerable responsibility for proving the abuse onto the child. At the same time, the view is being expressed that 'too many child protection inquiries result in too many children being interviewed' with the majority resulting in no criminal proceedings and 'too many civil proceedings fizz[ling] out due to the flawed nature of the evidence' (Hoyal, 1995: 319). As Summit (1983) has illustrated, disclosure is not the norm for a child who is likely to find it extremely difficult to talk about abuse, particularly if it has occurred within the family and Bacon

(1991) reminds us that disclosure is a process and not a one-off event. The guidance on the use of the *Memorandum* is conflicting and reflects the conflict between adult agendas and the interests and needs of the child. Objective, non-suggestive interviewing techniques are recommended as crucial to ensure that the evidence presented is not flawed and can be used effectively in criminal proceedings. The *Memorandum* states that 'the basic rule is that the interview should go at the pace of the child and not the adult' (Home Office, 1992: para. 2.18) but also 'strongly [recommends] that interviews are conducted in one day if at all possible' (para. 2.20). The advice to guardians *ad litem* is that 'when a child has been interviewed more than once, the court may attach less weight to interviews carried out subsequently, subject to expert advice' (Department of Health, 1995: 68). This inconsistent guidance highlights problems for the child who is thought to have been abused. Child-centred practice is described by Richardson and Bacon (1991: 24) as 'making a space in which children are listened to and believed and their interests protected in a way which allows them to feel safe and trusting enough to unburden'. Whether the *Memorandum* facilitates child-centred practice is questionable.

The *Memorandum* stresses the importance of planning and those conducting the interview must consider the position of the child in determining first whether to interview, the most appropriate people to conduct the interview and then the content and process of the interview and post-interview issues. In some situations civil proceedings will have been commenced and the guardian *ad litem* appointed before the *Memorandum* interview has been undertaken. In such situations, the guardian must ascertain the investigation and interview proposals and the likely effect on the child of interviews. The guardian will want to ensure that the needs of the child are fully recognised, that the plan is based on the interests of the child, and to make representations to the agencies involved if it appears that it is not. The guardian will also want to find out whether the child has sufficient understanding to give informed consent to any interviews. This is a crucial issue and will be explored further later in the chapter.

The experience of Kelly (aged 4) illustrates some of the issues arising from the use of the *Memorandum* in an investigation of non-accidental injury, where the responsibility for proving the abuse was placed with the child and the consequences for her were not fully considered by the professionals. Kelly sustained serious bruising to her head which was unexplained by her parents. Medical evidence was obtained which suggested that the injury had been caused non-accidentally by an adult. Although she was only four years old, the police wished to interview Kelly and her parents agreed. During the interview Kelly said that both her parents had caused her injury. Social services commenced care proceedings and the video was used as evidence in the civil proceedings. After initiating criminal proceedings, the police decided not to pursue them on the basis that Kelly was too young to with-stand cross-examination and that her verbal evidence was central to the prosecution. Kelly's parents denied the allegations and rejected Kelly for 'telling lies' about them, refusing to have contact with her or to allow her contact with her siblings.

There are clearly some children for whom the formal structure of inter-view(s) required by the *Memorandum* would be inappropriate and oppres-sive. Children whose first language is not English and those who have communication disabilities should only be interviewed if skilled interpreters are available and children who are seriously emotionally disturbed or very young will need protection from an investigation process which may rein-force their experience of abuse and powerlessness. The rights and needs of the child must be given priority, and the professionals must be prepared to defend their decisions, on the basis of the child's needs, against the require-ments of the courts which increasingly expect video interviews to be pro-vided in evidence. Anna's situation illustrates the conflicts between the child's rights and interests and the requirements of the courts. Anna (aged 2), a withdrawn and uncommunicative child was found to have signs of sexual abuse during a routine medical examination. Anna appeared to be unhappy, her behaviour was disturbed, with frequent temper tantrums and screaming. Anna's parents refused to believe she had suffered any abuse so social services commenced care proceedings and a guardian *ad litem* was appointed. Following discussions between the police, social services and the guardian, it was decided not to set up a *Memorandum* interview. The police decided not to commence a criminal prosecution as there was no evidence from Anna, which was considered to be essential to any prosecution. During work with a psychologist, approved by the civil court, Anna began to com-municate information about her abuse and her abuser. However, because this had not been obtained according to the *Memorandum* it was not accepted as reliable and the court subsequently hearing the case was critical that a *Memorandum* interview had not been undertaken. Those advocating on behalf of the child must be prepared to safeguard the child's rights and needs even when doing so may result in no reliable evidence being obtained.

Consent

The issue of consent is controversial and fundamental to any consideration of children's rights, with conflicting legal rulings about a child's right to give or withhold consent in matters of concern to them. The *Memorandum* states:

> where a child is mature enough to understand the concept, he or she should be
> given an explanation of the purpose of the video recording so that the child is fully

informed to a level appropriate to his or her age and understanding and freely con-
sents to the interview session and the video recording ... when the child is too
young to understand fully, the team should listen to the views of the parent or
carer (Home Office, 1992: para. 2.29)

Fundamental to the issue of consent is information. No one can give
informed consent to something they do not understand, or something that has
not been represented accurately to them, and they cannot properly consent if
they are subject to undue influence. The powerlessness of children who are
the subjects of child abuse investigations must be fully recognised by professionals if they are to give the child information in a way which the child can
understand and to offer a real choice about giving or withholding their consent to the interview and the video recording. The needs of children whose
first language is not English and children with disabilities must be recognised to ensure the provision of appropriate information which will enable
them to give or withhold informed consent.

It appears that in many situations children who give their consent do so
without full knowledge of what will happen to the video, which court proceedings it will be used in and the often very large number of people who
will see it. The child must be informed that they will lose their right to confidentiality, that they will have little control over the information they share in
the interview and that their views about any action to be taken against the
alleged perpetrator of the abuse will carry little weight. If the child's consent
is to be genuinely sought, these issues must be addressed and not evaded or
minimised. The pressures on a child to retract their statements after an interview can only be increased if they are not accurately informed and they do
not fully understand the consequences of giving their consent to both the
interview and the video recording.

The same principles must apply when professionals seek consent for the
video interview to be used for training purposes. The *Memorandum* states that
videos must not be used for training purposes unless 'specific and informed
consent has been given for that purpose, preferably by the child himself [sic]
... consent should not be sought before the interview, nor will it always be
right to do so immediately afterwards' (Home Office, 1992: para. 4.17).
Although some practitioners would argue that it is necessary and appropriate to seek such consent following an interview, from a children's rights perspective it is difficult to defend. Before the conclusion of any civil
proceedings, the guardian *ad litem* will want to check whether such consent
was sought and, if given, whether the views of the child have changed.
Charlotte (aged 13) was asked to consent to her video being used for training
at the end of her interview, and she gave it. Following criminal and civil proceedings which lasted 18 months, she was desperate that the video should be
destroyed and that no one else should see it. It may be that such consent

would be more appropriately sought following the conclusion of any court proceedings, rather than following the interview.

Confidentiality

The right to confidentiality in trusted, professional relationships is taken for granted by adults but there is confusion and conflict about whether this right should be afforded to children. Children are themselves confused about whether their wish for confidentiality will be respected. It is clear from the experience of ChildLine that children seek confidential advice and that they are more likely to confide problems if they can maintain some degree of control over what happens subsequently. The guidance suggests that 'the degree of confidentiality will be governed by the need to protect the child ... confidentiality may not be maintained if the withholding of information will prejudice the welfare of the child' (Department of Health, 1991: 13). The view of the official solicitor that 'a child ... should be told of the extent to which information ... is likely to be disseminated ... and the likely consequences. Such a child should be entitled to say that such information should be disclosed in a limited way or not at all' (Butler-Sloss, 1988: 25) is compelling. The child can be empowered within the *Memorandum* interview if interviewers are able to give them some degree of control over the information they are sharing which will contribute positively to their sense of their own worth and their ability to protect themselves.

Experts

While the guardian needs to have a good understanding of the *Memorandum* in order to assess the quality of the interview and the ability of the interviewers to understand and empower the child, a recent judgement (Re N (a Minor)(Child Abuse: Evidence) (1996) adopted earlier guidance in defining the limit of the guardian's expert role:

> The guardian should not attempt to appear in court as an expert witness in matters on which he [sic] is not competent and credible in the court's eyes as this can only undermine the child's case. The guardian is expected to be an expert in general child care matters not an expert in specialist areas (Department of Health, 1992: 40).

The credibility of children, particularly very young children, as witnesses is a contentious issue. Their right to be heard and believed, the reliability of their memory and their suggestibility has been the focus of considerable debate and dispute. Increasingly in civil proceedings where video evidence is presented expert psychological or psychiatric evidence is sought on the quality of the interview and the truthfulness and reliability of the child. The introduction of additional experts can have serious implications for the child, and the guardian's role as advocate for the child and mediator between the child and adults is crucial. The child's views on further assessments must be sought and their right to give or withhold their consent to any assessments directed by the court (s.44(7) Children Act 1989) must be represented to the court and respected. The potential for conflict between the needs of the court for further information and advice and the needs of the child for protection from unnecessary investigations and for privacy is considerable.

Court hearing(s)

The court world is adult, powerful, largely male and an intimidating place, even for many professionals, who view giving evidence with trepidation. An understanding of power relationships is essential for any appreciation of the position of the child entering this world. Support and preparation are crucial if the child is to survive what is a traumatic experience without suffering further abuse.

Charlotte's experiences illustrate some of the difficulties. Charlotte (aged 13) alleged sexual abuse by her stepfather and was interviewed according to the *Memorandum*. Her mother refused to believe her, so Charlotte was accommodated with foster carers. The police prosecuted Charlotte's stepfather. The case took 11 months to come to trial during which time Charlotte remained with foster carers but she was refused permission for therapy. Charlotte appeared in court and was subjected to cross-examination which amounted to a personal attack leaving her feeling confused, humiliated and worthless. Her stepfather was acquitted. Charlotte's mother insisted on Charlotte's return, which was against her wishes, so social services commenced care proceedings. Charlotte was overwhelmed with fear and anxiety at further court proceedings, the video interview being seen by more people and the prospect of being disbelieved and discredited all over again. Charlotte's experience of the court as abusive lends weight to Hoyal's (1995: 320) view that 'the welfare of the abused child should be paramount at all times even if that means a suspected abuser avoids prosecution or trial. If the trial cannot guarantee the child victim a high prospect of being believed, the prosecution should not proceed'.

Children who are involved in criminal and civil proceedings simultaneously may well experience confusion as different principles and practices prevail in the different jurisdictions. In civil proceedings, the child is unlikely to give evidence and whether they will be allowed to attend the hearing will be determined by the court. The higher courts discourage children's attendance on the basis that it is not in their interests to hear evidence which may be distressing for them. It seems that this view may be influenced more by the needs of the adults to protect themselves from the child's distress than by the needs of the child, who will have lived through the distressing events. A recent ruling advised that 'the presence of children should not be encouraged to develop into settled practice' (Lyon, 1994). The guardian *ad litem* has a duty to advise the court regarding the child's attendance and must be prepared to justify any recommendation that the child should be present. The guardian must advocate for the child in this matter, encouraging the court to be more child focused in the organisation and conduct of the case to include the child who wishes to attend. An essential aspect in empowering the child is to enable to child to participate in decision making on matters of concern to them and to be seen and heard. Newell's argument is compelling: 'if the child has to accept the outcome of the court's proceedings surely they have a right to be there ... if courts are to treat children as people not objects of concern, then having the child there may be vital' (1988: 204).

Conclusion

This chapter has sought to illustrate some of the issues for children and the guardians *ad litem* who represent them arising from the use of the *Memorandum* in civil proceedings. There are inescapable contradictions in the current systems in safeguarding the rights and interests of the oppressed, traumatised child and at the same time obtaining from them sound, unflawed, reliable evidence which will satisfy the requirements of the criminal court. Even where the interviewers are skilled, experienced in communicating with children and the agenda is focused on the child's best interests, the task may prove impossible within the formula of the *Memorandum* and the structure and practices of the criminal court.

A child's right to be listened to and to have his or her views taken notice of is generally accepted in principle, if not in practice. However, the child is dependent on the ability of the adult to communicate with them, to hear and understand their perspectives and to act on their views. The powerlessness of the child and the oppression they experience must be understood by professionals and agencies involved in child protection if they are to effectively protect children.

Although it has been suggested (Jackson, 1988) that the court rather than the child is the guardian's primary client, I would argue that the guardian must see themselves essentially as an advocate for the child, to empower the child to exercise their rights and to express their views within the powerful, patriarchal, legal and professional systems of the adult world in which they find themselves. The warning of Richardson and Bacon (1991: 148) that 'reluctance to be pro-active on behalf of children leads to an acceptance of an orthodoxy which best serves adult agendas', has resonance here where the multiple adult agendas are powerful and potentially further oppressive of the child. Guardians *ad litem*, of all people, must be pro-active in empowering children. As an independent professional fulfilling a complex role, the guardian is vulnerable to the pressures operating in the professional and legal systems. They must understand their own position in relation to these adult systems and the power relationships operating within them, actively challenge the conflicts in the system and empower themselves. The guardian *ad litem* occupies a unique and privileged position, with the opportunity and a heavy responsibility to promote and advocate for practice which truly empowers the oppressed child to be seen and their wishes and views to be heard, in an adult world where justice for children remains contentious.

References

Bacon, H. (1991), 'Cleveland's children: seen but not heard', S. Richardson and H. Bacon (eds) *Child Sexual Abuse: Whose Problem?*, Birmingham: Venture Press.

Butler-Sloss, E. (1988), *Report of the Inquiry into Child Abuse in Cleveland*, London: HMSO.

Davies, G., Wilson, C., Mitchell, R. and Milsom, J. (1995), *Videotaping of Children's Evidence: An Evaluation*, London: Home Office.

Department of Health (1991), *Working Together Under the Children Act 1989*, London: HMSO.

Department of Health (1992), *Manual of Practice Guidance for Guardians* ad litem *and Reporting Officers*, London: HMSO.

Department of Health (1995), *A Guide for Guardians* ad litem *in Public Law Proceedings Under the Children Act 1989*, London: HMSO.

Fox Harding, L. (1991), *Perspectives in Child Care Policy*, Harlow, Essex: Longmans.

Franklin, B. (1986) (ed.), *The Rights of Children*, Oxford: Basil Blackwell.

Frost, N. and Stein, M. (1989), *The Politics of Child Welfare – Inequality, Power and Change*, Hemel Hempstead: Harvester Wheatsheaf.

Holton, J. and Bonnerjea, L. (1994), *The Child, The Court and The Video: A Study of the Implementation of the 'Memorandum of Good Practice' on Video Interviewing of Child Witnesses*, London: Department of Health.

Home Office (1989), *Report of the Advisory Group on Video Evidence*, Chairman Judge Thomas Pigot QC, London: Home Office.

Home Office and Department of Health (1992), *Memorandum of Good Practice on Video Recorded Interviews with Child Witnesses for Criminal Proceedings*, London: HMSO.

Hoyal, J. (1995), 'In practice. The child, the court and the video', *Family Law*, 25, June, 319–20.

Jackson, C. (1988), 'The independent guardian *ad litem?' Family Law*, March 1988, 84–85.

Jones, J. (1993), 'Child abuse: developing a framework for understanding power relationships in practice', in H. Ferguson, R. Gilligan and R. Torode (eds), *Surviving Childhood Adversity*, Dublin: Social Studies Press.

Lyon, T. (1994), 'Case management – the Statutory framework', unpublished paper presented to IRCHIN/DOH Conference, July.

McNay, M. (1992), 'Social work and power relations: towards a framework for an integrated practice' in M. Langan and L. Day (eds) *Women, Oppression and Social Work*, London: Routledge.

Moore, S. (1993), 'Not angels, not devils, just kids', *The Guardian*, 26 March, 11.

Newell, P. (1988), 'Children's rights after Cleveland', *Children and Society*, 13, 199–206.

O'Neill, O. (1992), 'Children's rights and children's lives, *International Journal of Law and the Family*, 6, 24–42.

Richardson, S. and Bacon, H. (1991), *Child Sexual Abuse: Whose Problem?* Birmingham: Venture Press.

Solomon, B. (1987), 'Empowerment: social work in oppressed communities', *British Journal of Social Work Practice*, May, 79–81.

Summit, R.C. (1983), 'The child sexual abuse accommodation syndrome', *Child Abuse and Neglect*, 7, 177–93.

5 No easy answers: children's perspectives on investigative interviews

Amanda Wade and Helen Westcott

Critical appreciation of evidential interviewing has grown considerably since the introduction of the *Memorandum of Good Practice on Video Recorded Interviews with Child Witnesses for Criminal Proceedings* (Home Office, 1992). Why, then, do we need to consider children's perspectives? First, because the reformed procedures for obtaining children's evidence, to which the *Memorandum* contributes, developed without any *direct* input from children themselves. Secondly, the opinions of children involved in investigative interviews can inform and improve practice, by increasing adults' understanding and empathy. Practitioners rarely receive direct feedback from children in their day-to-day work, relying primarily on their own interpretation of the child's experiences. It is easy for these interpretations to be wrong, or to miss subtle cues from the child, as Butler and Williamson (1994: 51) illustrate in this example from an interview with a 16 year-old girl, raped by her stepbrother at the age of 11:

> Interviewer: So presumably being raped was the worst thing that has ever happened to you?
> Young woman: It was bad, but not the worst. The worst was when my stepbrother held me still – he used to get extra pocket money off my dad for helping him hit me – and my dad broke all my fingers, one by one.

Finally, and perhaps most importantly, we need to take account of children's views since it is their *right* to be listened to. Article 12 of the United Nations' Convention on the Rights of the Child (1992) reiterates children's entitlement to express an opinion on matters affecting them, and to be heard in any judicial or administrative proceedings. For these (and other) reasons, a growing number of child protection specialists are seeking out children's accounts of their experiences. Before we present our own findings (details of the research on which these are based can be found in the Appendix at the

51

end of this chapter), we will briefly summarise some recent studies in this area.

The literature on children's perspectives

Authors have principally reported that the organisational requirements of investigative agencies, and the needs of the criminal justice system, are prioritised over the needs of children (Barford, 1993; Wattam, 1992). This is reflected in professionals' failure to consult with children, or to give them meaningful choices in what happens, such as where or when interviews take place, or who is present (Barford, 1993; Roberts and Taylor, 1993; Wattam, 1992; Westcott, 1995). Further, children report being unprepared for these interviews, and having little prior information or explanation.

Evidential requirements dictate the nature of the interview, such as the manner of questioning and the particular questions asked. Children have complained that they do not always understand interviewers' language, and that the continual quest for specific details such as times and dates, leads to their feeling disbelieved. It is often not possible for children to remember such details (Blagg, 1989; Prior et al., 1994; Roberts and Taylor, 1993; Wattam, 1992).

Children like interviewers who are caring, listening, and who have a sense of humour. They want sensitivity, support, understanding, non-judgemental advice or explanations, trust and confidentiality. Conversely, children do not want to be interviewed by professionals who are lacking in these qualities, or who seem uninterested, uninvolved, or who trivialise or over-react (Barford, 1993; Berliner and Conte, 1995; Butler and Williamson, 1994; Prior et al., 1994; Westcott, 1995). It is important to children that they feel believed, and that interviewers recognise the depth of feelings aroused by their abuse and by the interview itself. Several authors have commented upon the degree of fear and anxiety experienced by children involved in investigations (Berliner and Conte, 1995; Roberts and Taylor, 1993).

These findings suggest there are tensions between children's needs and those of the system designed to protect them (see also Chapter 4). Our own studies offer further evidence of this.

What precedes the interview

We began by asking children about their involvement in the decision to formally report abuse. We found that the routes by which children come to the attention of investigators are many and various, but that it is rare for children to have any significant control over this process, irrespective of whether they have made a disclosure, or have not complained of abuse at all.

Children interviewed as a result of their own disclosure frequently described having first spoken out in circumstances of intense pressure. For some this pressure was internal and emotional, for others it was a result of external events or demands, or a combination of both:

> I cracked up at school because I kept seeing him in town and at the bus stops and he used to follow me home and I just had enough of it and I just cracked up and told one of the teachers at school (16 year-old girl).

> It was something I was bottling up ... I was always bottling it up. And it used to come to a time when I hated Thursdays and Wednesdays and he used to always go up to me Auntie's and ask if I were there ... I was going to school on the Friday morning and I didn't want to phone me dad up because I didn't know what he'd say and I didn't want to tell me nanna 'cos I didn't know what she'd say, so I told me cousin and then me cousin says 'Go on, Diane, tell our nanna.' So I told me nanna in end (11 year-old girl).

> I had no choice. I'd told my best friend about it and her mum found a letter I'd written her, and she said I'd got to tell my mum. If I hadn't told my mum by the end of the weekend, she said she'd tell her herself (14 year-old girl).

In disclosing their abuse, it was unusual for children to have any clear objective in mind other than sharing an experience which was distressing or intolerable. Some disclosed unintentionally:

> Well, I didn't think there were owt wrong with it at first. 'Cos I didn't understand. I were only ten and I didn't understand things like that. I didn't know owt about that stuff, like. It all happened with this ... Dave. We were at Junior Club and somebody says he were going to get a stripagram for his birthday and that's when I come out with it, like. And I goes ... I just sat there laughing, 'cos I didn't think there were owt wrong with it, and I said [...] and this woman that works there heard and she says 'What's that you said? Come over, into corner and tell me.' It just came out accidentally, like. I wouldn't have said owt because ... me mum always says 'Keep your gob shut. Stop saying things'. But it actually came out. I understanded then. We came home, and me mum didn't shout at me or owt for saying that (12 year-old girl).

Where children confided in a family member, it was usually the child's carer who reported the abuse to the authorities, and in most cases this was done in the expectation that an investigation would follow. However, some parents told us they had not intended to initiate an investigation; rather, they had wanted help for their child. Others had initially tried to make their own arrangements to protect their children from further abuse, but found, when seeking the provision of services such as re-housing or legal advice, that they came under pressure to report the abuse. In circumstances such as these children and their carer(s) often felt they had become involved in a process over which they had little control.

Similar feelings were experienced by children who first spoke of their abuse to a teacher. Some who sought help at school did so anticipating an investigation, but these were a minority whose expectation was based on the experience of peers or on television programmes. Many children described being quite unprepared for the investigation which followed their disclosure, and the speed with which the investigation began took them by surprise. A 14 year-old girl explained:

> After I'd told my teacher it all happened so fast. I just wasn't ready for it. I needed more time to sort myself out, my head was all confused. I didn't know what was happening or what I wanted or what I could do.

If a sense of bewilderment and anxiety was experienced by many children who had disclosed their abuse, this was even more the case when children were interviewed who had made no prior complaint. Some children suspected that the abuse was about to be reported:

> When it first got reported I was in school and I suddenly got called up ... I knew it was going to be coming anyway because my older sister wanted to report it as it was really getting to her and she talked to the counsellor often. [But] I didn't really like it being almost sprung upon me because I had no news about going to have this interview and statement done that morning. No, actually I remember getting a note to come to the counsellor saying that I would have to be there for second lesson but I was just told to be there and that someone was coming to see me (17 year-old girl).

However, others knew nothing until they were interviewed. An 11 year-old described thinking the police and social services wanted to talk to her because she had been looking after her younger siblings and was under age:

> They'd told me mum about it but they didn't tell me anything. I didn't know what were going off. At first I thought what it were about were ... There were like two things. I knew people could get in prison and there are people called social workers for under-age people looking after kids. I was looking after me sisters and I thought that were it. Then they told me in car that Georgie had been saying stuff and I says 'Ah, right'. So, I knew what it were about then.

Does it matter how far the children concerned have been involved in the decision to report their abuse? Some would argue that what is important is that children are protected, and any abuse identified and brought to an end. Indeed, many children spoke of the relief they felt when their abuse was in the open. However, together with the way in which the investigation is conducted, we believe it has implications for the extent to which an investigation is successful, and for the longer term outcomes for the child.

How the interview was conducted

The speed with which an investigation began, and the frequent lack of warning children received, was experienced by many children as stressful. A 9 year-old girl, interviewed twice, described her first interview as being worse than giving evidence at court, as she knew nothing about where she was being taken or why, until she reached the video suite:

> The first [video] they made, I didn't really tell them everything … I didn't know what was happening and what it was about … I didn't even know she was a police lady until I got there. If they would have told me before I even got there then it wouldn't really have been upsetting, but it was when I got there that I found out. That was what got to me.

Similarly, a 13 year-old boy commented: 'they come without us actually knowing. I reckon that was a bit surprising. It didn't help much'.

Most children said that they would have liked more time before they were interviewed, saying they needed to find out what the investigation involved and to understand its implications for themselves and their family. They also wanted an opportunity to get to know their interviewers, in order to feel comfortable with, and confident in, them. An 18 year-old commented:

> I was just sort of shoved in the room and interviewed, really. I was introduced but I wasn't, I didn't really feel very comfortable at first … I didn't want to speak to them because I didn't know anything about them and you know – complete strangers. I didn't know whether I could trust them or not.

Children thought insufficient attention was given to finding out how they felt about being interviewed, or discussing their anxieties. While most received an explanation of the purpose of the interview, the focus was usually on the practical issues involved, and this information was often described by children as having been given during the journey to the interview suite, or following their arrival there. Children did not always fully understand the information they were given or the implications of giving a statement. Where they understood that their allegations might lead to a court case, a common misapprehension was that the video recording would avoid the need for them to appear in court.

It was rare for children to have been consulted about the arrangements for the interview; most said they were not asked how they felt about its timing, location, or who was present. In some cases the option of a video recorded statement was not given, either because investigators trained in *Memorandum* interviewing were unavailable, or because of a temporary fault on the video recording system. When children gave written statements in these circumstances they could feel let down and were sometimes left wondering why the interview was not postponed.

The interview arrangements and manner in which it was conducted contributed significantly to alleviating or exacerbating children's anxieties. Children whose interview was held in a specialist suite invariably valued the comfort and privacy this afforded. However, the most important issue for children was who was present during the interview (particularly regarding mothers). Where this was discussed with children, or they were given the opportunity to be accompanied by a trusted person, they found this helpful, but a lack of information or attention to their feelings heightened their anxiety:

> I would have preferred it if [friend] was there because she knew all about this lot and they thought if she was in there then she'd have put things in me head ... I says, 'Is it alright if I have someone in with me?' and they said no in case the other stuff (16 year-old girl).

> I was a bit nervous ... about who was going to talk to me, what sort of things they was going to ask me. And who was on the other side of the booth, watching the video. They come and said a few things to me. Told me what they was doing ... told me social worker was there [behind the one-way mirror] but ... that was her. I didn't know who else was sat there with me social worker. Maybe there wasn't anybody, I don't know (14 year-old girl).

Many children were preoccupied during the interview with the likely effect of their statements on their family. Some were concerned to protect relatives from what they had to say, while for others speaking out felt risky and frightening:

> I was still fairly shaky and scared and I was worried that what I was saying was sort of, like, the wrong things. I often wished I hadn't started what I'd said, well, I just thought what were the consequences, now I have started the allegations. I always thought like, what would my mum say when she finds out, and half of me was relieved that I'd told eventually after three years and another half of me thought am I doing the right thing, should I have just kept my mouth shut and carried on, cause I knew I'd be bringing up a lot of bad feelings and I just didn't know if I was saying the right things (17 year-old girl).

> I were crying and running about saying I wanted toilet because I was a bit ... I was scared. Every time a car went by, a blue car, I kept on bobbing up and down think-

ing it was him. I'd got worries about what would happen, I'd got worries what me mum would do to me, and worries what he'd do to me. I felt safer in one way but I felt not safe in another. I felt like, me mum would get to me. Me mum would say, 'It's all a pack of lies and you'd do owt to get rid of him.' Which she did say; she says it was a pack of lies 'cos she wouldn't have thrown me out otherwise (11 year-old girl).

Preoccupations such as these made it difficult for children to concentrate on what they were being asked, and the questions themselves could tax them, compounding the embarrassment, distress and fear aroused by speaking of the offences. Although some children were able to describe a 'rapport' stage, the majority saw their interview as dominated by questions from the interviewer(s). At times the emphasis of questions confused children, making it harder for them to give an account of their experiences. This was especially so when interviewers sought specific details such as times, dates, clothing or sequence of actions:

[They were asking] what he were wearing, what I were wearing, what he said ... everything I could remember really. And I'm thinking – 'Well, was he wearing that? Or was he doing that? Or did he say that?' ... It just confused me a lot of the time ... I felt a bit intimidated at first by them because like, I were sat and like, they were asking me all questions and I were getting flustered. Because they needed to know and some of things I couldn't answer for them (17 year-old girl).

Because she was like, say like you pick a pin up and then put it in a pile of pins and it's sort of, pick *that* pin up, you know, and it was like it had to be the way, you know, and I couldn't remember (16 year-old girl).

Some children experienced interviewers as kind or supportive, but for others the interviewer's manner was off-putting. Interviewers who communicated disbelief, or who were experienced as non-empathic or manipulative, had an inhibiting effect on the children:

Because what I disliked about him, he made me feel I were lying when I knew full well I wasn't. He would say, 'Are you sure now you're telling the truth, 'cause if you're not, you know you'll be seriously in trouble.' He said 'These are very strong accusations you're making and you're not adding bits on are you? And making it sound worse than it is?' But he put me off from saying the real truth, really, in a way. I did tell the truth but he made me feel like I wasn't telling the truth so I got all me story muddled up in the end, because he was sort of chopping and changing me words in a way (17 year-old girl).

I would have found it easier talking with just the one person who were friendly, but when he came in [second interviewer], I just seemed to close up. You know, I just ... I didn't want to talk about it with him. He was ... trying like, little tricks and that lot, to try and see if I'm not telling the truth and that. And after a bit it was getting on my nerves (17 year-old boy).

[B]ecause of the way they were just like, blunt, or something, I couldn't say the whole story and I never did and I never will (17 year-old boy).

How children responded to the interview

The abuse reported by the majority of children we spoke to resulted in a prosecution, indicating that the information they had provided satisfied the sufficiency of evidence test applied by the Crown Prosecution Service. Nevertheless, many children told us that the account which they had given when interviewed was incomplete. They attributed this to the difficulty of talking about their abuse; lack of knowledge about what was happening; anxiety about what the investigation would lead to; concern that what they would say would cause distress to people they cared for; the stress of the interview itself; or their dislike of the interviewer. The implications of this are considerable, as the following case illustrates. Sally described herself as having been sexually abused by her stepfather from the age of 7. She eventually confided in her school teacher when she was 12. An interview was immediately arranged and conducted with Sally's mother sitting behind a one-way mirror, where she could see and hear the interview. This arrangement had not been discussed with Sally, who felt responsible for her mother's shocked and distressed reaction when informed of Sally's allegations. During the interview Sally was preoccupied with the possible effects of her disclosure on her family, and gave only a disjointed account of a single incident of abuse. However, a medical examination found physical signs consistent with her allegation, and a prosecution followed. Sally's stepfather pleaded not guilty and at his trial the video recording of Sally's interview was used as her evidence-in-chief. She was then cross-examined and, questioned about there having been only one incident of abuse, related another incident. In his final summing-up, defence counsel cast doubt on the initial allegation and the subsequent allegation in court, as follows:

The video interview:
All she said in the video interview, if it is true, is that there was one incident when her stepfather [attempted intercourse]. Now, if this man is perverted, you would have expected some course of conduct wouldn't you? But according to her account there was only one occasion when he behaved indecently towards her.

The allegation made in court:
Out of the blue today came another allegation – that only weeks before the video was made he [indecently assaulted her] in front of her mother, who was also on the

sofa. This is nonsense. It took us all by surprise, the prosecution included. My learned friend says, 'Well, she is a child. Be compassionate.' I apologise for sounding facetious, but she was asked questions by a trained police officer and was pressed on the matter: 'Has anything else happened?' 'No', she said. She says now that she didn't want to distress her mother. But she had already spoken of intercourse. It surely wouldn't have slipped her mind, especially if it happened only a few weeks before the video was made. Either it emphasises the fragility of a child's mind, or the murky waters we are getting into.

Sally's father was subsequently acquitted by the jury after a short deliberation.

The children and young people we spoke to are among those whose investigations are adjudged a success yet, while many talked of feeling relief when their abuse was in the open, more than half reported having mixed feelings after the interview. The social and economic costs of disclosure for many children and their carers was high. Few families received any active support once the investigation was concluded and only a minority had ongoing social work help. Thus many carers felt they and their children were abandoned once the investigation was completed and saw it as concerned solely with identifying evidence for a prosecution. Not all the children or their carers would have welcomed professional support after the investigation; nevertheless, the paucity of ongoing support was striking.

Children and the *Memorandum*: implications for policy and practice

The issues raised by children in our studies point to the existence of tensions between the needs and rights of children, and procedures for investigating child abuse. These tensions can be ascribed to the prioritisation of the requirements of the criminal justice system over the needs of children, and can be related to the guidance contained in the *Memorandum* or the way in which this has been interpreted in practice.

The *Memorandum* emphasises in its introduction that its guidance is not a universal prescription but rather a resource: 'each child is unique and the effective interview will be one which is tailored to the child's particular needs and circumstances'(Home Office, 1992: 1.). However, practitioners' concern to avoid accusations that children's accounts have been influenced or contaminated by those interviewing them has contributed to a close adherence to the *Memorandum's* recommendations. From the child's perspective this is of doubtful value where the *Memorandum* is based on an inadequate understanding of the disclosure process. Particular problems arise in relation to the timing of the interview; the planning which precedes it; the manner in which it is conducted; and the services available to children and their carers on its conclusion.

Timing

The *Memorandum* acknowledges the limited value of interviews which are conducted too early (Home Office, 1992: para. 1.7: 6) but defines this in terms of professional consultation and planning rather than the needs of children. Once investigators have had the opportunity to agree a plan of action the emphasis should be on speed: 'it is vital to proceed quickly. This will minimise the stress experienced by the child and reduce the risk of him or her forgetting important details, or being influenced by others' (para. 1.9: 6). From the child's perspective, however, the speed with which an investigation is conducted and a formal interview carried out can be problematic. Far from reducing the stress of the investigative process, swift action which fails to take sufficient account of children's feelings and wishes can exacerbate their difficulties. Many of the children to whom we spoke had made no disclosure of abuse at the time they were interviewed, or had made their disclosure under some form of stress and without an informed understanding of what would follow. What children need at this point is an opportunity to reach an understanding of the options facing them and to come to terms with the responses of those closest to them. Children experienced a range of conflicting feelings which at certain times made them want to speak openly and at others spurred them to minimise or disclaim their allegations. Evidential interviews which are premised on disclosure as an event rather than a dynamic process through which children move (Sorenson and Snow, 1991), and which are conducted too early in this process from the child's perspective, are likely to be characterised by tentative and incomplete statements, which may later be used to undermine a child capable of providing credible court testimony, as we have shown.

Planning

The *Memorandum* lays great emphasis on planning, but conceptualises this in a way which effectively marginalises the child and makes planning exclusively an issue for the professional. The interview strategy should '[draw] on all the skills and experience of the disciplines represented on the joint investigating team ... Professional help, for example from an educational psychologist or a teacher, may be invaluable to the team' (Home Office, 1992: paras 2.1 and 2.3: 9). The child is not referred to as being in any way a party to this planning process but 'can be informed about the substantive interview as soon as it is planned' (para. 1.8: 9). The *Memorandum* lists in some detail factors which interviewers should take into consideration, with the focus on identifying the child's level of cognitive, linguistic, social, emotional, physical and sexual development. Only a brief reference is made to assessing the child's state of mind and reaction to the investigative process, and there appears to be an underlying assumption that this can be addressed by experienced professionals without the necessity for any direct contact with the child him- or herself (para. 2.8: 10). We accept that broad generalisations can be made about children's 'likely' responses to the investigative process. However, as we have shown, the child's individual state of mind and motivation to participate in the interview will influence the account which he or she gives. If evidential interviews are to be successful in their objectives, greater attention to pre-interview contact with children is a pre-requisite. Not only will this ensure that issues which are significant to children are addressed on an informed basis, but it will help guarantee children an explanation of the purpose of the interview and the opportunity to discuss its possible outcomes. Most children to whom we spoke felt inadequately prepared for the interview; this invariably had consequences for their level of participation and for the completeness of their statements.

Conduct of the interview

The *Memorandum* does not anticipate sufficiently the real difficulties children encounter when giving an account of abusive experiences. One of the major issues to emerge from our research relates to the anxiety experienced by children during and after the investigative interview. There can be no doubt that the interview is perceived as emotionally charged. While the *Memorandum* briefly acknowledges the guilt, anxiety and feelings of responsibility which children may have (Home Office, 1992: para. 2.8: 10) and the discomfort they may experience when asked about abusive experiences (para. 3.14: 17), it offers few strategies to assist either interviewers or interviewees. There is an acknowledgement that a 'very young or distressed child' may benefit from being accompanied by a supportive adult during the interview (para. 2.27: 13) but there is no recognition of the support which a chosen familiar person can offer to children not falling into these two categories, nor of the indirect contribution he or she can make to the quality of the evidence the child provides (Moston, 1992).

Interviewers are advised to adopt a neutral demeanour to avoid communicating belief or disbelief in the child's allegations (Home Office, 1992: para. 3.8: 16) and thus compromising the credibility of the child's statements. Although the *Memorandum* accepts that children may at times need reassurance (para. 3.14: 17), interviewers may be reluctant to respond empathically as this can result in lawyers arguing that children are being rewarded for offering specific types of information. The difficulties inherent in attempts to reconcile the needs of children and those of the criminal justice system are illustrated by the fact that children to whom we spoke described interviewers whose behaviour they found supportive or kind, as having been of considerable assistance in helping them to speak of their experiences, while those who took the more neutral stance advocated by the *Memorandum,* were sometimes described as inhibiting or disbelieving.

The other significant problem reported by children in relation to the conduct of interviews appears to be one of *practice.* Many children depicted their interview as dominated by questions from the interviewer, and a search for specific detail which the children had experienced difficulty in providing. We accept that clarity, and the quality of the information obtained, are of vital significance for evidential purposes, but the type of interview described by children is not that recommended by the *Memorandum.* The underlying principle informing the interview strategy the *Memorandum* proposes, is that the most reliable information given by children is that which they spontaneously recall in a free narrative account (para. 3.12: 17). Interviewers are advised to resist the urge to ask questions, employing these primarily for purposes of amplification or clarification. Possibly the *Memorandum* underestimates the difficulty practitioners face putting this advice into practice, although it acknowledges that free narrative accounts may at times be unforthcoming, brief, confused, or unspecific. The invariable description by children of the interview as essentially an interrogation suggests this may be an issue for further training.

Aftermath of the interview

The mixed feelings reported by many children indicate that there are both positive and negative aspects to interviews from the child's perspective. Children felt better for having spoken of their experiences and having brought them into the open, but worse because they felt guilty, bad, or were concerned about the reaction of others. For a number, feared consequences proved a reality. The lack of support experienced after the investigation, and the impact of feelings of abandonment expressed by a number of children or their carers, should not be underestimated. Other studies have similarly highlighted the problems which arise when child protection investigation becomes a discrete activity focusing on the pursuit of evidence to determine whether abuse has occurred, while neglecting the wider evaluation of the child's overall welfare (Department of Health, 1995). There is a growing recognition that a criminally focused investigation may not be in the interests of every child, although for some it will be unavoidable.

In conclusion, we suggest that children's perspectives on the investigative process and the evidential interview raise issues for the criminal justice and child protection systems, and point to limitations in the *Memorandum.* For those within the criminal justice system the issues relate to the balance to be achieved between the interests of children and those of justice, while for those responsible for child protection they are concerned with the extent to which we are willing to allow children a voice in the decisions which affect them. In its focus on technique, and its relative inattention both to children's rights, and to the individual meanings which the investigation and interview can have for them, the *Memorandum* reinforces the risk that children will continue to be treated as 'objects of concern' (DHSS, 1988). Many of the children to whom we spoke felt that they had no control over the actions of professionals caring for them. Yet they had very clear ideas about the help they would have liked. Children have the right to be well prepared for the evidential interview; to be given an explanation of what will happen and to discuss the possible outcomes; to express a choice about who will be present; and to receive more emotional support. Are these incompatible with evidentially sound practice?

Acknowledgements

The authors would like to express their appreciation to all the children and young people who agreed to share their experiences. Amanda Wade's study was made possible by the financial support of the Wingate Foundation.

References

Barford, R. (1993), *Children's Views of Child Protection Social Work*, Norwich: University of East Anglia.

Berliner, L. and Conte, J. (1995), 'The effects of disclosure and intervention on sexually abused children', *Child Abuse and Neglect*, 19, 371–84.

Blagg, H. (1989), 'Fighting the stereo-types – "ideal" victims in the inquiry process', in H. Blagg, J.A. Hughes and C. Wattam (eds) *Child Sexual Abuse: Listening, Hearing and Validating the Experiences of Children*, Harlow, Essex: Longman.

Butler, I. and Williamson, H. (1994), *Children Speak: Children, Trauma and Social Work*, Harlow, Essex: Longman.

Department of Health (1995), *Child Protection: Messages from Research*, London: HMSO.

Department of Health and Social Security (DHSS) (1988), *Report of the Inquiry into Child Abuse in Cleveland 1987* (Cm 412), London: HMSO.

Home Office and Department of Health (1992), *Memorandum of Good Practice on Video Recorded Interviews with Child Witnesses for Criminal Proceedings*, London: HMSO.

Moston, S. (1992), 'Social support and children's eyewitness testimony', in H.

Dent and R. Flin (eds) *Children as Witnesses*, Chichester: Wiley.

Prior, V., Lynch, M. and Glaser, D. (1994), *Messages from Children: Children's Evaluations of the Professional Response to Child Sexual Abuse*, London: NCH Action for Children.

Roberts, J. and Taylor, C. (1993), 'Sexually abused children and young people speak out', in L. Waterhouse (ed.) *Child Abuse and Child Abusers: Protection and Prevention*, London: Jessica Kingsley.

Sorenson, T. and Snow, B. (1991), 'How children tell: the process of disclosure in child sexual abuse', *Child Welfare*, 70, 3–15.

United Nations (1992), *Convention on the Rights of the Child Adopted by the General Assembly of the United Nations on 20 November 1989*, London: HMSO.

Wattam, C. (1992), *Making a Case in Child Protection*, Harlow, Essex: Longman.

Westcott, H. L. (1995), 'Perceptions of child protection casework: interviews with children, parents and practitioners', in C. Cloke and M. Davies (eds) *Participation and Empowerment in Child Protection*, London: Pitman Publishing.

APPENDIX

The children and young people whose experiences form the basis of this chapter participated in two separate research studies undertaken by the authors. Brief summaries of these studies are provided below. For further details contact the authors directly.

Amanda Wade: 'The child witness and the criminal justice process: a case study in law reform', thesis in progress, University of Leeds
This study followed all cases involving evidence from children and young people dealt with over a seven-month period at one Crown court centre. All but one were cases of child sexual abuse. Twenty-six children, including both witnesses and complainants, agreed to take part in research interviews. The 21 girls and 4 boys were aged between 7 and 18 years when the interviews were carried out. Cases had taken between 12 and 24 months to reach the Crown court.
    Research interviews addressed the children's experience of the provisions for child witnesses introduced by the 1988 and 1991 Criminal Justice Acts, exploring their perceptions of the criminal justice process from investigation to post-trial. Interviews were carried out approximately 6 weeks after the conclusion of each case in the Crown court, and took place between February 1994 and January 1995. The children were aware that the researcher had observed the trials and so knew details of their case. Twenty-one interviews were also carried out with parents and carers.

Helen Westcott: 'Sexually abused children's and young people's perspectives on investigative interviews, *British Journal of Social Work*, 1996, 26, 451–74
Fourteen children and young people were interviewed about their experience of investigative interviews for suspected child sexual abuse, all of which had occurred prior to implementation of the Criminal Justice Act 1991. The children and young people were aged 6–18 years at research interview and 5–16 years at investigative interview; 9 were female and 5 male. In most cases the victim had disclosed their abuse and for 11 children there had been a criminal prosecution against the alleged abuser.
    The research interviews were held during November 1992–June 1993. Questions covered all aspects of the investigative interview: how it started, what happened in it, where it was held, who was present. Children were also asked how they felt about the interview process and about their interviewers. None of the questions probed details of the abuse itself; this information was obtained from case files.

6 The *Memorandum* and disabled children

Ruth Marchant and Marcus Page

This chapter is based on joint work involving two specialist facilities located close together in East Sussex: Chailey Heritage, a centre for children with physical and neurological impairments and Clermont Child Protection Unit, a service for the investigation, assessment and treatment of child abuse. Both centres operate within the public sector. Our combined experience is in working with abused and disabled children and young people, and teaching and consulting on issues relating to child protection and disability.

Since 1989 we have been directly involved with a number of children with different impairments who have been through child protection procedures, often including an interview conducted in line with the *Memorandum of Good Practice on Video Recorded Interviews with Child Witnesses for Criminal Proceedings* (Home Office, 1992). This has included physically disabled children, children with sensory impairments and children with different degrees of learning difficulties. Most have had multiple impairments. We have interviewed children using a range of augmentative and alternative communication systems (primarily British Sign Language and symbol or word-based communication boards accessed in different ways). We have also interviewed children with receptive and expressive language disorders and children with speech impairments. In the majority of these interviews we have used communicators or interpreters.

This chapter offers a guide to the main issues to address when planning a *Memorandum* interview for a disabled child. We first set the context; considering definitions of disability and the 'created vulnerability' of disabled children, and looking at the broader social and political context in which the *Memorandum* was introduced.

We believe that disabled children should have the same rights to justice and protection as all children. This means ensuring that their communication needs are recognised to enable them to give an evidentially valid account of any abuse which they have experienced.

Clarification of terms used

Within the disability movement, definitions and language are recognised as important because they construct our understanding. Many disabled people use the term 'disability' not to refer to impairment (functional limitations) but rather to describe the effects of prejudice and discrimination: the social factors which create barriers, deny opportunities, and thereby disable people (e.g. see Morris, 1995). This perspective contrasts with the strong medical emphasis of many of the dominant definitions, including that within the Children Act 1989, which was used to ensure the inter-relation of all legislation concerning disabled children.

For the purposes of this chapter we are using, as far as possible, the social definition of disability, and from such a perspective it becomes clear that in many instances the child protection system can further *disable* the children with whom we are concerned, because it has usually been designed by non-disabled adults for non-disabled children, and this may be reflected in policies, facilities, and practice.

In line with this perspective we refer to 'disabled children' rather than 'children with disabilities' as this phrase is preferred by many groups representing disabled people. When discussing specific communication difficulties we emphasise the two way nature of communication. We use the term *communication* to describe any form of interpersonal exchange; *language* to describe formalised systems of symbols, words or signs and *speech* to refer to the physical production of word sounds. *Communication boards* are augmentative systems used primarily with children who cannot speak, and consist of symbols/pictures/photos/words that represent the child's expressive vocabulary.

The social and political context

The last few years have seen a growing awareness of the prevalence of the abuse of disabled children, together with a recognition that this is linked to the general oppression of disabled people, manifest in social policy, services and at a personal level (see, for example, Westcott, 1993; ABCD Consortium, 1993; Sobsey, 1994; Kennedy, 1996 and Westcott and Cross, 1996).

This recognition that disabled children may be placed at increased risk of all forms of abuse, both within families and within services, contrasts with an apparent under-representation of disabled children within the child protection system. Disabled children may also face other forms of discrimination such as racism or sexism. This 'multiple jeopardy' can have a double effect: increasing the risks of abuse and reducing the chances of protective intervention.

Uncertainties in the professional system create further vulnerability. The *Memorandum* was introduced in the midst of major organisational change, when many authorities were relocating their services for disabled children to their children and families divisions, in line with the emphasis within the Children Act 1989 on disabled children as 'children first'.

The Social Services Inspectorate (1994) report on services to disabled children and their families noted two areas of concern in relation to this relocation of services: an anxiety that the detailed knowledge and the expertise and skills of specialist workers would be lost and a fear that services for disabled children would be accorded a lower priority than children for whom local authorities have other statutory duties, particularly child protection (Social Services Inspectorate 1994: para. 5.11.9). Our experience suggests that such fears are well founded: the transfer of responsibility away from specialist teams has often meant that workers without prior experience in the field of disability are expected to have or acquire the necessary competence without additional training or support. This is compounded by the lack of regular, relevant training in child protection offered to those working with disabled children. The professional divide we described earlier thus continues (Marchant and Page, 1993).

Specific effects of the *Memorandum*

Some authorities have taken the opportunity to improve protection services for disabled children by creating joint specialisms. However, the majority of local authorities and police forces have developed new structures and procedures which reflect the increasing 'criminalisation' of child abuse (Bentovim et al., 1994). Largely as a result of the Criminal Justice Act 1991 and the *Memorandum*, which emphasise the collection of evidence for criminal investigation, the police now frequently take the lead role in investigating child abuse and interviewing children. Within this context, the protection of disabled children may be compromised, for at least three reasons.

First, the threshold for a formal investigative interview has been raised. Prior to the *Memorandum*, this threshold was defined by the principles and practices established through various child abuse inquiries (Butler-Sloss, 1988); through *Working Together* (Department of Health, 1991a), and judgments in the High Court. Whereas a video recorded interview would once be conducted in instances of suspected child sexual abuse it is now more common for such an interview to be thought appropriate only when a child has made a specific allegation. Disabled children may face additional barriers in making allegations. Allegations are much less likely when a child has a restricted social understanding, when their access to personal safety information is limited or non-existent, when they have restricted access to the necessary vocabulary or when their account is less likely to be believed or reported (see Kennedy, 1993; Marchant and Page, 1993).

Secondly, the competence of a child witness is now assessed on more restrictive criteria. The *Memorandum* encourages investigating teams to take a bold view of the issue of competence, and to 'assume that the courts will be willing to listen to the evidence of any child who is able to communicate about the alleged offence in a way the team as a whole can understand' (Home Office, 1992: para. 2.14). However, the difficulties in practice of securing convictions against perpetrators of child sexual abuse have led to a much more restrictive interpretation being applied by the Crown Prosecution Service and this influences police decisions about which child witnesses to interview. This may impact more heavily on disabled children, particularly as there is no opportunity in criminal proceedings to educate a judge and jury about a different method of communication or to ensure that language used by barristers is appropriate to the developmental level of the disabled child or young person.

Thirdly, there may be no alternative to a *Memorandum* interview. In terms of the criminal process, the decision not to interview under *Memorandum* guidance may be well founded on developmental or psychological considerations, but it can still be vital for the child's protection and welfare to establish whether abuse has occurred and who was responsible in order that a child's welfare and care needs can be planned for. The nature of such 'assessment' interviews (see Bentovim et al., 1995) is more child-centred and facilitative in style, but they may still be admissable in the civil courts. However, in some social service departments, when it has been decided that an interview under the *Memorandum* is not appropriate, there may be no alternative procedure for conducting a video recorded interview with suitably skilled and trained interviewers.

It has been our experience that assessment interviews have often proved essential in formulating effective protection plans for disabled children and, in cases of abuse by care staff or other professionals, the video recorded evidence has been very influential in disciplinary proceedings and avoided the need for a child witness to be reinterviewed by the different interested parties.

Preparation for a *Memorandum* interview

Referrals of disabled children can disrupt the usual child protection processes. The number of agencies and workers involved with most disabled children means that communication needs to take place across professional boundaries. Roles may be uncertain and there may be confusion about the allocation of tasks, and specialist advice or assistance may be needed from professionals unfamiliar with child protection. Thus planning for interviews of disabled children may take considerably longer than for non-disabled children (see Marchant and Page, 1993; Page, 1995). The following areas need particularly careful consideration.

Creating a safe environment

The physical setting of the interview needs to provide a feeling of security and safety for both the child and the interviewing team. Unfortunately, limited resources have often combined with limited disability awareness to create inaccessible facilities, despite the statement in the *Memorandum* that 'facilities need to be suitable when children have a hearing or mobility disability' (Home Office, 1992: para. 1.14). For a child whose health is fragile, it is important to avoid unnecessary stress and to take account of the likely distress which may be caused by the recall of abuse. Usually the child and his or her parents or other carers are in the best position to inform those planning the interview about the child's health needs, but sometimes it may be necessary to seek medical advice or even to arrange for a qualified health practitioner to be present at the interview or to be on standby for assistance.

Communication issues

The *Memorandum* refers to the need to take account of a child's 'apparent developmental stage ... taking an overview of cognitive, linguistic, emotional, social, sexual, physical and other development', and it also states that 'knowledge of the child's linguistic development is particularly important' (Home Office, 1992: paras 2.3, 2.4). Impairments affect a child's development in different ways. Some impairments have little or no effect on a child's communication, while others have effects which may not be immediately apparent. For example, many sensory and physical impairments will impact widely on a child's general learning about the world and language development: a child who is physically unable to manipulate objects is likely to have an insecure grasp of verbs and prepositions, as these are generally learnt by children through performing actions themselves. Speech and language therapy advice should be sought at the earliest possible stage and when requesting such advice it is necessary to be specific about the nature of the interview and how questions might be framed to satisfy evidential requirements.

Choice of interviewer

The balance of knowledge and skills needed for interviewing disabled children – in terms of both disability and the evidential requirements for child protection – are rarely found within one individual. Many experienced interviewers can feel very anxious and doubt their own competence when faced with a child whose communication method is unfamiliar to them. Our experience suggests that the lead interviewer should be experienced in conducting *Memorandum* interviews, but have the openness and sensitivity to accept advice and assistance from a person who is expert in the child's form of communication and particular condition. This second person may also take on the role of communicator for the child, or act as an observer and co-supervisor. 'Communicator' refers here to a person who assists with the child's communication, whereas the term interpreter is used to refer to a qualified spoken or sign language interpreter (see Kennedy, 1993).

The involvement of a communicator or interpreter adds to the preparation time needed, whether English is the child's second language, or the child communicates through sign or uses another alternative method or has a speech impairment.

The interview

The *Memorandum* states that 'the effective interview will be one which is tailored to the child's particular needs and circumstances' (Home Office, 1992: para. 1.3), and interviewers are encouraged to 'develop effective strategies for the interview to minimise the effect of a speech or hearing or learning disability...' (para. 2.10). However, as Westcott (1994: 29) notes: 'It will be crucial ... to demonstrate that the interview was planned this way to meet the child's needs and that variations from the *Memorandum*'s approach are not post-hoc decisions that result from poor interviewing technique.'

The following comments are based on our experiences of attempting *Memorandum* interviews with children whose impairments affect their communication.

Phase one – rapport

The rapport phase is essential in determining the overall quality of the interview. Research suggests that surprisingly little time is given to children in general for this rapport phase (Davies et al., 1995, found an average of 7 minutes). In our experience with disabled children, rapport phases that last 30–40 minutes are not unusual. Establishing rapport between the interviewer and the child may in itself require more time and attention, especially if a third person is needed to assist communication.

Additionally, where the child's impairment affects communication, the rapport phase has other important functions, such as to relax and inform the interviewer, to educate the viewer about the child and their impairments and to dispel some common myths and prejudices (for example, that physical impairments inevitably affect a child's intelligence). It can help to focus on the child's abilities, and thereby increase credibility and build the child's own self-confidence. Disabled children may be very used to dealing with low expectations of their intellectual abilities, and welcome the opportunity to prove what they can do. It is particularly important to allow the child to demonstrate their method of communication and their ability to understand. This will be central in determining the child's competence as a witness. It is also important for the child to sense the importance of communicating clearly, and for the interviewer to develop as much skill as possible in talking with and understanding the child.

During the rapport phase the recording of the interview can be adjusted if necessary to ensure that the child and any accompanying adult can be heard and seen and that any communication aids are audible and visible. The roles of observer, supervisor and technician may be best separated if possible, to ensure the highest possible quality of recording. It is useful to bear in mind that any difficulty that the interviewer or observer has in understanding the child's account at the time is likely to be magnified for any person subsequently viewing the video recording. The interviewer needs to be comfortable about referring to this and asking the child to repeat, rephrase or clarify as needed.

The rapport phase should also give the child opportunities to explain their world, especially where this might be unusual and relevant for the interview (if the child stays away from their family, if there are different adults involved with their care at home or elsewhere, if the child needs intimate care or other 'unusual' help in day to day life, etc.). It is important to establish the context at this stage to give meaning to what may follow as it is often harder to go back afterwards. If, for example, a disabled child has a number of adults involved in their care, it will be important to demonstrate their ability to distinguish reliably between these different people. Alternatively, if a child needs very invasive care procedures (for example, intermittent catheterisation) it will be helpful to establish the child's comprehension of this as a process before any discussion of possible sexual abuse ensues.

Establishing rapport with disabled children may require additional ground rules, for example clear expectations of any additional adult taking part in the interview. The initial introductions can be usefully supplemented with brief explanations of the expectations of those present, for instance by outlining people's 'jobs', for example the interviewer – to listen carefully to what the child has to say, and to ask questions; the communicator or inter-preter – to help the child and interviewer understand each other.

The rapport phase also needs to include the 'admonition to tell the truth', which may need particularly careful attention with disabled children, whose experiences may make them more compliant and eager to please adults (see Blyth and Milner, 1989) or may lead them to feel discreditable (Westcott and Cross, 1996). Some learning disabled children may also have difficulty understanding the concept of truth, and interpreted communication may lead to additional confusions. It can help if everyone in the room makes a commitment to tell the truth (including the interviewer and any additional adults). It is important to convey that it is also permissible for the interpreter to say 'I don't know how to say that' or 'I don't understand'; they must not guess if they are not sure.

Finally, disabled children may need very explicit permission to request breaks, and a clear simple sign, gesture or word with which to do so. Given the concentration required by all parties, it is important to establish that the adults can request breaks as well as the child.

Phase two – free narrative account

The risk of a too brief rapport phase is that the full competency of the child in the interview situation remains unclear to both the interviewing team and to any subsequent observer of that child's interview. Used correctly, the rapport phase should have established how well a child would be able to provide a spontaneous account of events and also give a child confidence that the inter-viewing team will not become impatient or critical if the child has difficulties in expressing what he or she means.

Impairments do not necessarily prevent a child from giving a spontaneous account, except possibly when a child is relying heavily on yes/no signalling, or using a restricted communication board that would make it difficult to introduce certain topics, or where a child has not reached the developmental stage of being able to tell a story (see Marchant and Page, 1993 for discussion).

The free-narrative account by the child should ideally provide a general map of the territory to be covered in the next phase, when it will be necessary to elicit and clarify the detail of what has been alleged. Commonly, a child will have given only a partial account and a learning disabled child may often require a greater degree of facilitation before it is clear whether or not there has been an offence or some form of abuse. If this is the case, open-ended prompts should be used as far as possible, for example: 'Can you think of a way to tell me more?'; 'Can you explain as much as you can about it in your own words?'; 'Can you think of a way to show what you mean?'; 'Can you say it another way to help me understand better?'.

Reflecting back to the child in an open, non-directive manner what she or he has told the interviewer helps to ensure accuracy as well as perhaps facilitating the telling of further details.

Phase three – questioning phase

The subdivision of this phase into four stages is in practice an artificial division, as interviewers will select which part of a child's account they wish to clarify first and may need to go through the different 'stages' with each part to achieve optimum clarity. In planning questions, the interviewing team needs to be aware of factors which may be relevant for forensic purposes, for example:

- Disabled children may be dependent on others for intimate care. Interviewers will need to be able to distinguish between necessary caring or medical procedures and abusive or criminal actions.
- Children may be receiving orthopedic treatment or using postural management equipment that might cause temporary pain or discomfort but should never cause injury.
- A child's condition may restrict the positions he or she can get into or be placed into and some positions may in themselves be dangerous.
- Certain physical or neurological conditions are likely to affect the sensations a child can feel.
- A child with a sensory impairment may be restricted in some of the information they can provide about the identity of the alleged suspect or details of the alleged offences.

In all such situations, planning is essential to ensure that a child is not being expected to respond to questions they cannot answer, or asked questions that are inherently confusing. This is important not just in terms of the child's emotional welfare, but also in order to avoid undermining the child's credibility.

The most contentious category is without doubt that of the leading question, which is defined in the *Memorandum* as 'one which implies the answer or assumes facts which are likely to be in dispute' (Home Office, 1992: para. 3.51). A common misperception is that the *Memorandum* bans leading questions altogether. In fact, it states that

> as the courts become aware of the difficulties of obtaining evidence from witnesses who are very young or who have a learning difficulty ... a sympathetic attitude may be taken towards necessary leading questions.

It also states that

> 'a leading question which succeeds in prompting a child into providing information spontaneously ... will normally be acceptable' (Home Office, 1992: para. 3.54)

but adds the caveat that the interviewer should never be the first to suggest that an offence has occurred.

The optimism of the *Memorandum* in this matter of leading questions has not yet been borne out in practice. In some instances, the question and answer may be blanked from the screen in court at the order of the judge. The effect on the jury is not simply to deprive them of the information gained from the question but can undermine the credibility of the whole interview.We have argued elsewhere that with children using communication boards many questions need to be asked in a closed form – that is, with only a yes or no response necessary (Marchant and Page, 1993). Our more recent experience suggests that various questioning techniques can increase the evidential validity of closed questions.

The *Memorandum* suggests mixing up questions which seek a yes and no response, and seeking to revert to a neutral or open questioning mode to increase the chances of admissibility (Home Office, 1992: paras 3.31–3.35). In addition we would suggest framing questions such that less likely alternatives are suggested first (e.g. 'Was that touching nice?' before 'Did that touching hurt?'). Secondly, when asking a series of linked questions (e.g. 'Did x, or y or z touch you in a way that you didn't like?'), it is necessary to ensure that the series is completed rather than halting at the first positive response. When identifying a perpetrator of alleged abuse, any series of such questions should not commence or conclude with the name of a suspected party. Thirdly, when offering the child a range of alternatives, consistent wording is needed each time, particularly if the child has a learning impairment or poor short-term memory.

Phase four – closing the interview

As there is generally so little experience of *Memorandum* interviewing with disabled children, and given the tendency to believe that the process itself may be detrimental to their welfare, it is important to obtain feedback from the child on their experience of the interview during this closure phase, and perhaps also to acknowledge again the additional barriers that communication difficulties can present in terms of telling about abuse. Our experience is that children have often valued the opportunity to be listened to in such a careful way.

Conclusions

One risk of focusing on the *Memorandum* is to lose sight of the fact that it is only one part of a criminal justice system that is generally biased towards protecting the rights of the defendant, and which leaves many victims, both adults and children, further damaged. All abused children face enormous obstacles in obtaining justice within such a context, and these obstacles are magnified and compounded for disabled children.

Radical changes are needed throughout our criminal justice system if there are to be more successful prosecutions of crimes, particularly sexual crimes, against children. The hopes of many workers in the field of child protection were raised by the Pigot Report (Home Office, 1989), which had proposed that a child's evidence might be heard without the need for cross-examination in court. In the context of these hopes, the Criminal Justice Act 1991 has been extremely disappointing, particularly for disabled children. Few involved in child protection work, let alone disabled children and their parents, would subscribe to the view set out in the foreword of the *Memorandum* that 'the interests of justice and the interests of the child are not alternatives'. There are a number of myths that perpetuate the risks to disabled children: that disability protects children from abuse; that speech is the only valid way to communicate and that disabled children cannot be competent witnesses. Such myths will need to be repeatedly and confidently challenged in the next few years if disabled children are to be offered the same rights to protection as other children.

Inclusive, comprehensive child protection services which are able to genuinely adapt to each child's individual needs would have beneficial effects on practice with all children.

There is a value in offering children as evidentially sound an interview as possible, even if a criminal prosecution appears unlikely at the outset. The child's own account has value in formulating protection plans, in civil proceedings or in disciplinary action and can inform therapeutic work or the teaching of personal safety skills.

The *Memorandum* should not be permitted to become a straightjacket on interviewers nor for the stricter interpretation of the guidelines to become, in effect, a threshold which children have to cross before a referral for a video recorded interview is made, which would serve to further discriminate against disabled children.

It is important to acknowledge that there are some children with whom we do not yet know how to communicate about possible abusive experiences in ways which would be accepted as evidentially safe, or that would remove doubt from our own minds. At present this might include children with severe or profound learning difficulties, and children with autism and related disorders, but our experience over the last six years has been a gradual lowering of the threshold of children we consider it possible to interview.

Disabled children swim against many tides. We are beginning to realise that these include an increased risk of abuse and a reduced chance of protection. Working to the limits of the *Memorandum* it is possible to enable very many disabled children to give clear accounts of their experiences in ways which are evidentially valid. However, more far-reaching changes are needed in the criminal justice system if disabled children are to demonstrate their competence and credibility as witnesses within courts. The scales of justice are tipped against all child victims when the main evidence is their oral testimony, and they are undoubtedly tipped even further for children whose impairments affect their communication.

Acknowledgement

We would like to acknowledge the expertise and support of the multidisciplinary teams of Clermont and Chailey Heritage on whose combined work this chapter is based.

References

ABCD Consortium (1993), *Abuse and Children who are Disabled*, Reader and Resource Pack, Leicester: NSPCC.

Bentovim, A. (1994), 'Criminal obstacles to working in partnership', keynote address *BASPCAN Congress*, Bristol: BAPSCAN.

Bentovim, A., Bentovim, M., Vizard, E. and Wiseman, M. (1995) 'Facilitating interviews with children who may have been sexually abused', *Child Abuse Review*, 4, 246–62.

Blyth, E. and Milner, J. (1989), 'Compliance and abuse', *Special Children*, October, 8–9.

Butler-Sloss, E. (1988), *Report of the Inquiry into Child Abuse in Cleveland 1987*, London: HMSO.

Davies, G., Wilson, C., Mitchell, R. and Milsom, J. (1995), *Videotaping Children's Evidence: An Evaluation*, London: HMSO.

Department of Health (1991a), *Working Together Under the Children Act 1989*, London: HMSO.

Department of Health (1991b), *The Children Act 1989 Guidance and Regulations Volume 6: Children with Disabilities*, London: HMSO.

Department of Health (1995), *Messages from Research*, London: HMSO.

Home Office (1989), *The Report of the Advisory Group on Video Evidence*, Chairman Judge Thomas Pigot QC, London: Home Office.

Home Office and Department of Health (1992), *Memorandum of Good Practice on Video Recorded Interviews with Child Witnesses for Criminal Proceedings*, London: HMSO.

Kennedy, M. (1993), 'Human aids to communication', in ABCD Consortium, *Abuse and Children who are Disabled*, Reader and Resource Pack, Leicester: NSPCC.

Kennedy, M. (1996), 'Sexual abuse and disabled children', in J. Morris (ed.) *Feminism and Disability*, London: Women's Press.

Marchant, R. and Page, M. (1993), *Bridging The Gap: Child Protection Work with Children with Multiple Disabilities*, London: NSPCC.

Morris, J. (1995), *Gone Missing: A Research and Policy Review of Disabled Children Living Away from Their Families*, London: Who Cares? Trust .

Page, M. (1995), 'Investigating abuse when children have learning disabilities', *NAPSAC Bulletin*, No. 11, March, 3–7.

Sobsey, D. (1994), *Violence and Abuse in the Lives of People with Disabilities: The End of Silent Acceptance*, Baltimore, MD: Paul H. Brookes Publishing Company.

Social Services Inspectorate/Department of Health (1994), *Services to Disabled Children and their Families*, London: HMSO.

Westcott, H.L. (1993), *The Abuse of Disabled Children and Adults*, London: NSPCC.

Westcott, H.L. (1994), 'The *Memorandum of Good Practice* and children with disabilities', *Journal of Law and Practice*, 3 (2), 21–32.

Westcott, H.L. and Cross, M. (1996), *This Far and No Further: Towards Ending the Abuse of Disabled Children*, Birmingham: Venture Press.

7 Black children and the *Memorandum*

Anna Gupta

The aims of this chapter are to explore particular issues relevant to the use of the *Memorandum of Good Practice on Video Recorded Interviews with Child Witnesses for Criminal Proceedings* (Home Office,1992) when interviewing black children and to consider the implications for the development of anti-oppressive policy and practice. The subject areas addressed in other chapters are of relevance to all children, however because of the power relationships in British society it is crucial to consider specific issues for black children in order to ensure their rights and interests are taken into account when investigating allegations of abuse.

The term 'black' is used in this chapter to refer to people of African, African-Caribbean and Asian descent. Black people share a history of oppression as a result of colonialism and continue in British society today to experience racism because of the colour of their skin. It is essential to emphasise the great diversity among black people in Britain whose languages, religions, cultures and lifestyles differ enormously, while also recognising a shared experience of racist oppression. Macdonald (1991: VI) defines racism as being 'a belief that black people are inferior to white people in relation to their culture, religion, intellect, beliefs, lifestyles'.

In this chapter an examination of the use of the *Memorandum* in child abuse investigations involving black children is undertaken with the intention of highlighting possibilities for the development of anti-oppressive policy and practice. When describing the construction of anti-discriminatory social work, Langan (1992: 3) states that: 'It seeks to develop an understanding of both the totality of oppression and its specific manifestations as the precondition of developing an anti-discriminatory practice relevant to all spheres of social work.' In this chapter the term 'anti-oppressive' is used to describe what the above quote refers to as 'anti-discriminatory' practice. Although mainly used in a negative sense, the word 'discrimination' can have beneficial connotations, for example positive discrimination. Oppression can only be destructive.

Institutionalised oppression has been and continues to be a major force operating in British society. Power relationships based on domination and subordination occur along the dimensions of race, gender, sexual orientation, age, ability, class and employment/economic status (Jones, 1993). Oppression occurs at different levels, including the interpersonal, familial and structural and takes a variety of forms, such as material, emotional and ideological (McNay, 1992). Fundamental to any awareness of power relations is the acknowledgement of the interlocking nature of oppression.

Black feminists have played a crucial role in highlighting the importance of addressing the interconnectedness of different forms of oppression and the danger of creating a hierarchy. Collins (1990: 229) states:

> In essence, each group identifies the oppression with which it feels most comfortable as being fundamental and classifies others as being of lesser importance. Oppression is filled with such contradictions because these approaches fail to recognize that a matrix of domination contains few pure victims or oppressors.

Although this chapter focuses on racist oppression, it acknowledges that black children and their families experience a variety of other forms of oppression that must also be recognised by practitioners working with them. It is also argued that practitioners themselves must recognise their own experience of the multiple systems of oppression, their capacity for domination and victimisation in order to use their power to empower child victims and their non-abusing carers (Jones, 1993).

Throughout this chapter the impact of child abuse on black children living in a racist society is considered. The type of abuse that is examined in most detail is sexual abuse. Although the *Memorandum* can be used for interviewing child victims of other forms of abuse, it is most frequently used in cases involving child sexual abuse (Davies et al., 1995). Case examples are provided to illustrate some specific issues black children and families face when involved in child protection investigations.

Manifestations of racism

Racism is endemic in British society and permeates all aspects of life. The civil rights organisation, Liberty, submitted a report to the United Nations Committee on the Elimination of Racial Discrimination confirming that racial oppression figures in everyday life for millions of Britons (Liberty, 1996). The manifestations of racism vary from overt racial attacks, including murder, to more subtle, covert strategies that serve to deny black people employment, decent housing and other essentials, further reinforcing the power base of white people. Dominelli (1988: 8) argues that:

The unarticulated nature of racism makes it difficult for the majority of white people to see racism as an endemic feature of society, permeating all aspects of it. It also enables white people to perceive racism as the crude, irrational beliefs and actions manifest by a few National Front supporters instead of a normal feature of social interaction between black and white and acquire a self-concept which is not racist.

It is essential that any worker committed to investigating child abuse in a manner that upholds the child's welfare as being paramount begins to develop an understanding of racism and ways of challenging racist attitudes and behaviours.

Institutional, individual and cultural racism occur throughout the police and social services, the two agencies responsible for investigating child abuse in accordance with the *Memorandum*. Both agencies have many individuals who hold racist attitudes and act out racist behaviours towards colleagues and clients. The fact that these individuals remain either police or social workers indicates widespread collusion with racism. Senior management personnel in both agencies are predominantly white and although social service departments generally employ more black staff, the majority of staff are white (Langan, 1992).

Social services departments perpetuate racism by denying black people access to appropriate services such as placements for children that fail to address their racial, cultural, religious and linguistic needs and therapeutic services that do not acknowledge the impact of racism.

Social work assessments are frequently based on stereotypical generalisations about black people's cultural characteristics. Ahmed et al. (1986) argue that because of cultural racism there is a tendency to label most problems experienced by Asian girls as being a result of 'culture conflict'. Therefore a referral regarding behaviours, such as self-harm, that with a white child could be considered one of possible sexual abuse, is likely to be categorised as a conflict of culture when the child is an Asian girl. Modi and Pal (1992) stress the need for an Asian mother's behaviour to be analysed from the perspective of the family living in a hostile society. Failure to do so may lead to an inappropriate label of a 'collusive mother'. Black children are often subject to punitive responses leading to their being removed prematurely as well as non-intervention, when action is clearly necessary, as the workers fear being labelled racist (Jones, 1994).

The police tend to have even less awareness and training about issues of race than social workers. The existence of racist attitudes and behaviour within the police force and consequent mistrust of police by black communities is well documented. One example is highlighted in the Liberty report which stated that a black man is far more likely to be stopped and searched than a white man (Liberty, 1996). In her study of statutory and voluntary sector responses to domestic violence against black women, Mama (1989: 181–2) found ample evidence of police racism, including the example of Patience, a Nigerian woman who was subject to violent abuse by her husband. When the police were called on one occasion they ended up arresting her, keeping her in custody all night, ridiculing and racially humiliating her before releasing her without charge.

The differences in the training, awareness, value base, culture and ethnic composition of the staff groups between the police and social services may create difficulties in the joint working relationship. Racism, as well as other forms of oppression such as sexism and the powerlessness of children needs to be addressed in joint training programmes and continually by management and workers in order to minimise the negative consequences for service delivery.

Workers undertaking child protection investigations need to be aware not only of their own and their agency's policies and practices that perpetuate racism, but of the daily oppression experienced by black people and the impact of this on their lives. The 'colour-blind approach' is a common strategy that endorses racism. Colour-blindness advocates that all individuals are treated as if they were all the 'same'. Black people's experience of racism and other forms of oppression is ignored and little account is taken of the different cultural, religious and traditional practices of black people. On occasions when these differences may be recognised, they are viewed as inferior and expectations placed on black people to conform to white society and the stereotypes of blacks that abound (Dominelli, 1988).

Unfortunately, this form of racism is prevalent throughout the dominant theories that underpin practice with children who have been abused. There is a dearth of literature on the impact of abuse on black children and their experience of child protection interventions. Research on children's experiences of child abuse investigations undertaken by the NCH Action for Children (1994) across nine London Boroughs fails to mention the ethnic origin of the subjects and therefore to address any specific experiences of black children. A summary of Department of Health funded research admits that 'issues of race, gender and rights may not be as salient in the studies as readers might wish' (Department of Health, 1995: 6) . It is crucial that practitioners critically examine research within the context of an understanding of oppression.

In summary, in order for workers to be able to offer black children a child protection service that challenges rather than compounds the oppression they face, there needs to be an acknowledgement of different forms of racism that exist on structural, institutional and interpersonal levels. Both the police and social services departments must examine their recruitment procedures with the aim of employing more black staff. Once black staff are in post, agencies need to consider ways of both eradicating the racism faced by these members of staff and empowering them. Improving service delivery to black clients, whether it be via training for staff that encourages anti-oppressive practice, service provision that reflects black families' needs or taking seriously feedback from service users, must be a continuous goal.

Planning the investigation – the child's situation

The *Memorandum* stresses the importance of adequate planning and warns that failure to do so is likely to have a negative consequence for both the child and justice. The document delineates several key areas that should be addressed in the preparation of the plan, including the child's development; use of language; ideas about trust; state of mind; cultural background and any disabilities (Home Office, 1992: 9–10). This preliminary assessment of the child should be used to consider whether an interview is appropriate, the timing of the interview, personnel present, content of interview, as well as post interview protection and therapeutic issues. As the investigation progresses increasingly more information will be available about the child and the initial assessment should continually be reviewed.

Social workers and police officers need to draw on their knowledge base when planning the investigation and key theories regarding the impact of abuse on children and the difficulties children face during the process of disclosure are crucial in beginning to understand the child's situation. However given the prevalence of colour-blindness in mainstream academic theory, it is vital to consider the information within a context of oppression that includes the dimensions of race, age, gender and disability.

Finkelhor and Browne (1986) present a model of four traumagenic dynamics affecting the child who has been sexually abused: powerlessness, traumatic sexualisation, betrayal and stigmatisation. Unlike white children, black children frequently experience racist violence and abuse outside their home, so when abuse occurs within their family, their sanctuary from racism is violated adding to their insecurity, vulnerability and feelings of betrayal (Imam, 1994). The very experience of living in a racist society will have negative consequences for the black child's sense of self-worth and feelings of being able to control his or her environment. This is compounded by sexual and other forms of abuse which could result in black children being more prone to feelings of self-blame and stigmatisation (Jones, 1993).

Black children may also see the abuse as being caused by their blackness, which could inhibit their ability to develop a positive racial identity. Following abuse by her African-Caribbean father, Louise, a 9 year-old mixed parentage girl went to great lengths to deny her blackness, including cutting off all her plaits and covering her skin with Nivea cream. White children do not have to deal with this effect of abuse as their identity is not constantly assailed, but instead reinforced by positive role models.

Dobash et al. (1993: 122) found that abusers used 'coercive behaviour in which the victim is treated like an object devoid of separate personal emotions to be used for the sexual gratification of the perpetrator'. Black people are objectified also by racism and their human status is defined as less significant. In some circumstances this may result in black children being more vulnerable to abuse as in the following case example. Marcus (aged 7), Sally (aged 8) and Carol (aged 7) were the only black children at a holiday play scheme; they were also the only children to be abused by one of the white workers, who referred to their race in a derogatory manner during the abuse. These children had to cope with the effects of abuse that was of both a sexual and blatantly racial nature.

Children who are abused by offenders of the same sex are stigmatised by homophobic attitudes prevalent in British society. This is another form of oppression that black children who have been abused may experience. Some black children have also to deal with specific homophobic attitudes associated with their own community. For example, Islam regards homosexuality as an abomination (Osmany, 1991).

Most children find it difficult to disclose abuse, particularly that which has occurred within their family. For black children the difficulties and dilemmas are compounded by racism. The feeling that the child is betraying his or her community and perpetuating racist myths may inhibit a black child from disclosing abuse. A racist response by the police and criminal justice system may be feared, should the abuser be a person whom the child cares about. As Charmaine explains: 'I couldn't tell about my dad because I loved him and I didn't want him to get into trouble and I thought white people would make racist comments'(Rouf, 1991).

Denial and secrecy are pervasive themes relevant to all aspects of sexual abuse. Summit (1988) suggests that it is all of society, not just those immediately affected, that protects the secret of child sexual abuse. Patriarchy perpetuates denial for its own ends. Its manifestations include silence about the role of male power and the extent of abuse of this power (Macleod and Saraga, 1988; Hall and Lloyd, 1989). For black communities, the additional fear of further stigmatisation and pathologisation compound the forces of denial (Modi and Pal, 1992).

Summit (1983) identifies a typical pattern of behaviour that children adopt in order to survive the hostile responses from both the perpetrator and wider society. The 'Child Sexual Abuse Accommodation Syndrome' comprises five categories: (1) secrecy, (2) helplessness, (3) entrapment and accommodation, (4) delayed, conflicting and unconvincing disclosure, (5) retraction. Disclosure is a difficult and traumatic process for any child. By talking about his or her abuse, the child is challenging omnipotent adult male power. Not surprisingly, the account is often tentative and confused, which in turn is frequently responded to with reactions of disbelief and rejection. These confirm the child's feelings of powerlessness, guilt and shame and often lead to retraction of the disclosure. It is easier to maintain the lie and continue to experience sexual victimisation (Summit, 1983).

In order for workers to protect a child effectively and pursue the prosecution of an abuser they must constantly attempt to minimise pressures that could lead to a retraction either prior to or after an interview. It is crucial that the different dimensions of oppression, including race are addressed. Amina's story highlights some of these issues.

Amina is a 13 year-old Bangladeshi Muslim girl. She informed a teacher at school that she had been subjected to sexual abuse by an adult male cousin for a period of several years. She wanted the abuse to stop, but was very scared about her parents knowing and terrified that she would be taken into care and placed in a children's home where she would be the only Bangladeshi girl. Amina lives with her parents, siblings and paternal grandparents. At the time of her disclosure her father and grandparents were in Bangladesh for a family wedding.

A female social worker and police officer visited Amina's mother with a Sylheti-speaking interpreter. She was shocked and upset by Amina's disclosure, but believed Amina and was supportive of her. She and Amina consented to a video interview. During the interview Amina gave a clear account of serious abuse. After the interview both Amina and her mother were extremely concerned about the consequences of the disclosure. They had not informed Amina's father and were worried about his response. They were concerned about the shame this would bring on the family, particularly for Amina's grandparents who are also the grandparents of the abuser. They are an elderly couple whose life revolves around the local community and mosque. Their concern also extended to the young wife of Amina's cousin, who has only recently come to Britain from Bangladesh and has a baby. What would happen to her if her husband was sent to prison? There was also the question of whether knowledge of the sexual abuse would affect Amina's and her siblings' chances of a good arranged marriage.

Not surprisingly, a few days after the interview and prior to the arrest of her cousin, Amina retracted her allegation and stated that they wanted nothing more to do with social services or the police.

The non-abusing carer

The support of a non-abusing carer, who in cases of intra-familial sexual abuse is usually the mother, is vital for any child who has been abused. Not only can a mother's support be utilised in the physical protection of her child, but it is also crucial for a healthy resolution of emotional conflict. Children who are not supported and believed by their mothers are more likely to develop serious and long-term emotional damage (e.g. Goodwin, 1981, cited in Print and Dey, 1992: 57).

The role of the non-abusing carer is important throughout the investigative process. Carers can provide valuable information about the child when planning the interview; they can support the child prior to the interview and provide post-interview protection and care. However, workers must be sensitive to the needs of the non-abusing carer, particularly in situations where she has only recently learnt about the abuse. Print and Dey (1992: 70) suggest that: 'The effects on a mother of the sexual abuse of her child are comparable to those typically associated with bereavement ... shock and numbness, followed by denial, anger, guilt, resentment, isolation, sorrow, self-pity and finally acceptance.'

There are many manifestations of the power structures of our patriarchal society that inhibit mothers from being able to offer support to their children. Workers must address these power blocks on interpersonal and structural levels. When considering the role of a black mother, workers must be particularly cognizant of the impact of racial oppression. Black mothers like their children may be very wary of engaging the help of police and social services through fear of receiving a racist service (Mama, 1989). Iman's story highlights some of the difficulties black women face when attempting to protect themselves and their children from male violence in a racist society.

Iman is a Somalian woman with four young children. When pregnant with her fifth child she was subjected to a violent attack by her husband. Her eldest son was also injured. He was video interviewed and reported a catalogue of violence towards himself, his mother and siblings. Iman and her children were placed in a refuge on the outskirts of London as this was the only place available. Iman could not speak English and an interpreter was only provided by the local authority for a few hours each week. The rest of the time Iman had to communicate via her son. She found negotiating with schools, Department of Social Security and housing departments extremely difficult. The area was predominantly white and she and the children experienced racial abuse both in the refuge and outside. Because of limited financial resources and fear of meeting her husband, Iman was not able to visit her friends. After several weeks she became severely depressed. She was hospitalised and care proceedings were initiated on all her children. No criminal prosecution of her husband was pursued.

Religion and culture have been used universally by men to maintain their power over women and children. Black men are no different from other men when they use tradition to perpetuate the subordination of women and children. The concept of *izzat* or family honour is used by Asian men to control women, by linking it exclusively to women, who are considered the embodiment of family honour (Imam, 1994). The implications for some women and their children, who are viewed as defiling *izzat* and betraying their family and community by informing the authorities of abuse and leaving their partner, are great. Ostracism from their family and community has grave consequences for many black women as the alternative is isolation in a hostile and racist society.

Care must be taken by workers not to dismiss a culture or religion, even if they may find certain practices that subjugate woman and children abhorrent. Respect for other cultures can be shown in seemingly insignificant ways, such as not arranging non-urgent visits or interviews during religious festivals like Eid or Diwali, and using the name with the correct pronunciation that the client wishes to be called. On a broader level, community work could be undertaken with black women's groups that aims to empower them to challenge racist and sexist oppression, including the denial surrounding sexual abuse.

In any child protection investigation the planning process is vital and must involve an examination of the context of the child and her non-abusing carer's life. If professionals fail to explore the race and gender dimensions of black mothers' experiences and to offer sensitive help, their interventions may undermine the contributions black mothers can make to their children's participation in the investigative process and then subsequent safety and emotional recovery. Workers must be able to examine behaviour to understand which reactions may stem from coping strategies developed for survival in a racist society (Bernard, 1995).

The *Memorandum* interview

Consent

The *Memorandum* dictates that children and their families should be given an explanation of the purpose of the video recording that enables an informed decision regarding consent to be made. Barford and Wattam (1991: 96) argue that, although not intending to be dishonest, workers frequently do not pay sufficient attention to what may be relevant to the child and place a gloss on the truth in order to get the child to accept the situations they are placed in and thus avoid having to face the full extent of a child's pain. It is particularly important that black children and their carers are not further disempowered by lack of information when making a decision about consent. They have a right to detailed information and time spent answering their questions before informed consent can be expected from them. Written information and video or audio tapes that provide information on child protection procedures should be available in different languages. The NSPCC and London Borough of Tower Hamlets have produced a useful video in Sylheti with English subtitles for use with Bangladeshi families (NSPCC and Tower Hamlets ACPC, 1996).

Interview personnel

The *Memorandum* suggests that the interviewing team should consider, in light of the issues identified during the planning process, the best person to conduct the interview and who, if anyone should accompany that person. Given the powerlessness of children, particularly those who may have been abused, it is preferable that they be offered some choice about who interviews them. It is vital that girls from communities, such as Muslim communities, where sex is not openly discussed, have the opportunity to talk to a woman. It is likely that a male interviewer would increase their embarrassment and inhibit them from talking about sexual abuse.

Some black children may find feelings of betraying one's family and community lessened by being interviewed by a person from their community. Others may find it harder to talk to someone from the same cultural background (Phillips, 1993). Black children, however, are frequently not offered a choice as there is a dearth of black police officers and black people are underrepresented in social services. Khadj Rouf's (1991) experiences vividly describe the isolation many black children face: 'My social worker was white. The police surgeon was white and he was a man ... I felt very alone. I wish someone who understood my culture and abuse could have come and talked to me and my family.'

All interviewers need to ensure that the interview process considers the context of that child's particular life. This includes the use of toys and props that reflect the child's race and culture, and questions that respect rather than stereotype that child's background (Phillips, 1993).

Use of interpreters

The *Memorandum* recommends that the interview should be conducted in the child's first language, however it does not confer a right and does not address the complexity of offering a skilled interpretation service in the context of child abuse investigations. No member of the steering group that developed the document represented an interpretation service (Smith, 1993).

The rights of black and minority ethnic children whose first language is not English are severely reduced by a system that does not prioritise their needs. The training of interpreters is essential for children's rights to be upheld. Interpreters need to be familiar with the stages of a *Memorandum* interview and the particular types of questions used. A video interview with Lola, a Yoruba speaking girl, was rejected when an independent interpreter found that several leading questions involving the name of the alleged perpetrator had been used. It is also important for an interpreter to be aware of the impact of the language used on the child. For example, sex is not generally openly discussed in Bangladesh and the terms to describe sex or sexual organs in

Bengali are limited. Either they are very academic and beyond common usage or so crude and colloquial that they are offensive (Osmany, 1991). An interpreter is faced with the difficult task of deciding whether to use language that may be difficult for a child to understand or terms which further compound feelings of guilt and shame. According to the SSI report on the implementation of the *Memorandum*, only three authorities reported training language interpreters in evidential interviewing (Social Services Inspectorate, 1994: 35).

It is also vital that social workers and police officers are trained on the most effective use of interpreters. It is not easy to build a rapport with a child with whom you are not directly communicating. Given the difficulties associated with interviewing a child through an interpreter, it would be extremely beneficial if a nationwide register could be developed of workers who can interview children in different languages to a recognised standard.

The court process

The giving of evidence in court is inevitably a stressful experience for a child. The Social Services Inspectorate report on the implementation of the *Memorandum* stated that court experiences were seen as another form of abuse, especially as the defence frequently discredited child witnesses by undermining their self-worth and creating guilt and confusion (Social Services Inspectorate, 1994). Given that the judiciary and legal profession are dominated by white people, the court process is likely to be particularly traumatic for black children. Feelings of stigmatisation and guilt could be compounded for the child if they and the defendant are the only black people in court.

Davies et al. (1995) suggest training and information for the judiciary on good court practice in cases involving child witnesses will help minimise the trauma faced by children. Clearly any such training needs to include information on the needs of black children.

Conclusion

This chapter has sought to raise issues relating to the impact of racism on black children and their families involved in child protection investigations that include *Memorandum* interviews, with the aim of promoting anti-oppressive policy and practice. In order for the *Memorandum* to truly serve the interests of children and justice, racism must be addressed throughout the investigative process. However this cannot be undertaken in isolation and it is also essential that management are committed to eradicating racist practices within their agencies. The interlocking nature of oppression has to be recognised and other forms of oppression experienced by children and their families must also be challenged. If we are to offer protection to all children in Britain, individual workers must be supported by their supervisors and agencies within a society that is committed to eradicating racism, sexism, poverty and other forms of structural oppression.

References

Ahmed, S., Cheetham, J. and Small, J. (eds) (1986), *Social Work with Black Children and Their Families*, London: Batsford.

Barford, R. and Wattam, C. (1991), 'Children's participation in decision-making', *Practice*, 5 (2), 93–102.

Bernard, C. (1995), 'Childhood sexual abuse: the implications for Black mothers', *Row Bulletin*, Winter, 9–13.

Collins, P. (1990), *Black Feminist Thought: Knowledge, Consciousness and the Politics of Empowerment*, London: Routledge.

Davies, G., Wilson, C., Mitchell, R. and Milsom, J. (1995), *Videotaping Children's Evidence: An Evaluation*, London: Home Office.

Department of Health (1995), *Child Protection: Messages from Research*, London: HMSO.

Dobash, R., Carnie, J. and Waterhouse, L. (1993), 'Child sexual abusers: recognition and response,' in L. Waterhouse (ed.) *Child Abuse and Child Abusers*, London: Jessica Kingsley.

Dominelli, L. (1988), *Anti-Racist Social Work*, Basingstoke: Macmillan.

Finkelhor, D. and Browne, A. (1986), 'Initial and long-term effects: a conceptual framework', in D. Finkelhor et al. (eds) *A Sourcebook on Child Sexual Abuse*, Newbury Park, CA: Sage.

Hall, L. and Lloyd, S. (1989), *Surviving Child Sexual Abuse*, Hampshire: The Falmer Press.

Home Office and Department of Health (1992), *Memorandum of Good Practice on Video Recorded Interviews with Child Witnesses for Criminal Proceedings*, London: HMSO.

Imam, U.F. (1994), 'Asian children and domestic violence', in A. Mullender and R. Morley (eds) *Children Living with Domestic Violence*, London: Whiting and Birch.

Jones, A. (1994), 'Anti-racist child protection', in T. David, (ed.) *Protecting Children from Abuse*, Staffordshire: Trentham Books.

Jones, J. (1993), 'Child abuse: developing a framework for understanding power relationships in practice', in H. Ferguson, R. Gilligan and R. Torode (eds) *Surviving Childhood Adversity: Issues for Policy and Practice*, Dublin: Social Studies Press.

Langan, M. (1992), 'Who cares? Women in the mixed economy of care', in M.

Langan and L. Day, (eds) *Women, Oppression and Social Work*, London: Routledge.

Liberty (1996), *Human Rights and Racial Discrimination,* London: Liberty.

Macdonald, S. (1991), *All Equal Under the Act?* London: Race Equality Unit.

Mama, A. (1989), *The Hidden Struggle : Statutory and Voluntary Sector Responses to Violence Against Black Women in the Home,* London: London Race and Housing Research Unit.

Macleod, M. and Saraga, E. (1988), 'Challenging the orthodoxy – towards a feminist theory and practice', in *Feminist Review,* 28, Spring, 16–56.

McNay, M. (1992), 'Social work and power relations: towards a framework for an integrated practice', in M. Langan and L. Day, (eds) *Women, Oppression and Social Work,* London: Routledge.

Modi, P. and Pal, J. (1992), 'Beyond despair', in M. Winfield, (ed.) *Confronting the Pain of Child Sexual Abuse,* London: Family Service Unit.

NSPCC and Tower Hamlets ACPC (1996), *Protecting our Children,* London: NSPCC and London Borough of Tower Hamlets.

Osmany, N. (1991), 'Child sexual abuse and the Bangladeshi community in Tower Hamlets', in London Borough of Tower Hamlets, *Poplar Project: A Social Work Team's Account of its Work with a Group of Sexually Abused Young People,* London: London Borough of Tower Hamlets.

Phillips, M. (1993), 'Investigative interviewing: issues of race and culture', in Open University (1993), *Investigative Interviewing with Children: Trainers Pack,* Milton Keynes: Open University.

Print, B. and Dey, C. (1992), 'Empowering mothers of sexually abused children – a positive framework', in A. Bannister, (ed.) *From Hearing to Healing: Working with the Aftermath of Child Sexual Abuse,* Harlow, Essex: Longman Group.

Rouf, K. (1991), *Black Girls Speak Out,* London: The Children's Society.

Smith, G. (1993), 'Good practice or yet another hurdle: video recording children's statements', *Journal of Child Law,* 5 (1), 21–4.

Social Services Inspectorate (1994), *The Child, the Court and the Video,* London: HMSO.

Summit, R. (1983), 'The child sexual abuse accommodation syndrome', *Child Abuse and Neglect,* 177–93.

Summit, R. (1988), 'Hidden victims, hidden pain: societal avoidance of child sexual abuse', in G.E. Wyatt and G.J. Powell, (eds) *Lasting Effects of Child Sexual Abuse,* Newbury Park, CA: Sage.

8 The *Memorandum*: an international perspective

J.R. Spencer

The *Memorandum* is part of the scheme for taking children's evidence created by the Criminal Justice Act 1991. This was a 'watered-down' version of the proposals of the Advisory Committee on Video Evidence, alias the Pigot Committee (Home Office, 1989), under which the whole of a child's evidence (including cross-examination) would have been recorded on videotape ahead of trial, and under which certain children would have been questioned by a single, neutral examiner charged with putting the questions for both prosecution and defence.

Five years later it is worth asking two questions, both of which have an international dimension. First, how does the Pigot scheme, and its poor relation eventually enacted, compare with the ways in which children's evidence is taken in other jurisdictions? Secondly, how far can we go in changing the law to protect child witnesses in criminal proceedings without coming into conflict with our international obligations as contained in the European Convention on Human Rights?

Children's evidence in criminal proceedings in other legal systems

Broadly speaking, there are two main types of criminal procedure in the Western world: the accusatorial ones, as found in the English-speaking world, and the inquisitorial ones, as found in France, much of the rest of continental Europe, and various other countries whose laws have been influenced by the continental systems.

The idea behind the accusatorial system is a contest. 'A' makes an accusation against 'B' in front of a neutral judge (or judge and jury). The accuser calls his evidence, and the judge (or judge and jury) decide whether the accusation has been proved. The idea behind the inquisitorial system, on the other hand, is an official enquiry. Following an accusation the state nominates a trusted agent – the judge – to look into it. This person questions everyone, records their answers, studies the file, and on the file decides where the truth lies. Each type of system has its merits, and each one has its faults: and there are good versions and bad versions of each. Over the centuries, furthermore, the countries with inquisitorial systems discovered merits in the accusatorial system, and borrowed some of its ideas, while in some of the accusatorial systems the same has happened in reverse. In consequence, the line between the two types of system is no longer a clear one. Instead of being divided into two camps, the legal systems of the Western world are ranged across a spectrum: from mainly accusatorial systems, through completely mixed systems, to mainly inquisitorial systems which have imported some accusatorial ideas.

The inquisitorial systems

At present, among the systems that are most heavily inquisitorial are those of France and Holland. These have adopted the accusatorial idea to the extent that the court that finally determines guilt or innocence takes no part in the initial process of investigation. But for serious cases, they retain a major link with their inquisitorial tradition in the form of a person called in French the *juge d'instruction* – or in Dutch the *rechter-commissaris*. This person is a junior judge, who (among other duties) questions the defendant and the witnesses ahead of trial, usually after initial questioning by the police. This questioning session takes place in private. The defendant is not present, unless the *juge d'instruction* decides to arrange a confrontation between the defendant and the witness. The official record of one of these preliminary questioning sessions, and of any earlier formal questioning by the police, is called a *procès-verbal*. These *procès-verbaux* form part of an official file, the *dossier*, which is put before the court of trial. Broadly speaking, the contents of the dossier are – to put it in common lawyer's terms – part of the evidence in the case. If the witness testifies at the final trial, the court has the *procès-verbaux* to supplement his oral evidence, and if he or she does not, the *procès-verbaux* of the earlier questioning sessions can replace it. For French and Dutch judges, a *procès-verbal* is automatically a piece of evidence; the common law notion that such a record is inadmissible as hearsay, and that only oral evidence at trial can count, would seem to them an odd idea indeed.

In these jurisdictions there is anxious debate (as elsewhere) about the credibility of children's evidence, but they do not have the acute practical problems about putting a young or highly traumatised child's story before the court that arise in the common law world, where we insist on oral evidence, and reject almost everything else as hearsay. In France, a child witness would probably have been first questioned by the police, and then either by the *juge d'instruction* or by a person more experienced in talking to young children, to whom the task has been officially delegated by *commission rogatoire*. During one of these sessions the child would probably have been shown a video of the defendant, or confronted with the defendant in person. The record of all these questioning sessions would usually have formed part of the evidence at the eventual trial. In a sex case, furthermore, the child would typically be examined by a psychological or psychiatric expert appointed by the court, whose report – probably containing substantial helpings of what the child had said – would also be put before the court at trial. In Holland it would have been much the same.

The obvious question that an English lawyer would ask about this sort of system is 'What safeguards does it contain for the defendant?' These systems have traditionally provided certain safeguards. First, there are detailed rules as to how witnesses are examined in the pre-trial phase, and how their statements have to be recorded. Secondly, the defendant (and of course the prosecutor) has the right, in principle, to apply for any witness – including one who has previously been examined – to give live evidence at trial. From the defendant's point of view, however, this is less useful than at first sight it may appear. In Holland (although not in France) the court has the power to reject a defence application to call a witness to give live evidence. In many situations, furthermore, the *procès-verbal* of the original interview remains part of the evidence in the case even where the witness gives live evidence, even if he or she does so and retracts in the process. The defendant's opportunities for a hostile cross-examination are also limited by the fact that, traditionally, the questioning of the witnesses is carried out by the judge. Thus in many cases, neither prosecution nor defence will even attempt to exercise their right to call the child at trial. Furthermore, if a child – or adult – witness is summoned but fails to attend the trial, the presiding judge may allow the case to go ahead on the basis of the *procès-verbaux*.

A further safeguard is *la confrontation*. Where a witness accuses a suspect and the suspect denies his guilt, French (and to a lesser extent Dutch) legal tradition requires the *juge d'instruction* to arrange a confrontation between them. This means that the witness must attend a further private questioning session, at which he or she is asked to repeat the accusations in the presence of the accused. If the witness at this session retracts the accusation, this does not wipe out the previous statements, which remain evidence as part of the dossier: but it obviously weakens the weight that the court of trial is likely to put upon them.

In continental Europe, however, there is a growing feeling that these fairly minimal traditional safeguards are insufficient. In some jurisdictions there have been reforms with a view to establishing direct contact between the trial court and the witness, enabling the court to hear for itself what the witness actually said. In addition, there have also been moves to make sure that the defence have at least some possibility of challenging the accuser.

Changes designed to put the witness into direct communication with the court first took place in Germany. At one time the German rules about hearing witnesses were similar to those in France, but over a century ago they were modified to bring in a 'principle of personal examination' (*Grundsatz der persönlichen Vernehmung*). Article 250 of the current Code of Criminal Procedure provides that where evidence of a fact is based upon a person's observation, this person shall be examined at the trial, and the examination may not be replaced by reading the record or an earlier examination or a written statement. This means that in Germany, as in England, child witnesses must in principle give live evidence at criminal trials. In Germany, however, it is still easier than it is in England for the child's account to be put before a criminal court. First, an earlier statement can be used in evidence where it is impossible to produce the witness at the trial (and legal machinery exists to have a witness formally examined by a judge ahead of trial if he or she looks unlikely to be able to give live evidence when the trial takes place). Secondly, there is no general ban on hearsay evidence. Thus, for example, there is nothing to prevent a German parent telling the court what his or her child said the defendant had done. And when a German child does come to court he or she is not subjected to the sort of gruelling cross-examination that might take place in England, because in Germany the examination of child witnesses is invariably conducted, as in France and Holland, by the presiding judge (Frehsee, 1990). Some German courts have also been experimenting with 'live links' to spare the child having to testify in the courtroom.

Much more recently, important changes in the way the legal system deals with children's evidence have come about in Holland. In response to public criticism of the way in which children were currently being questioned by court-appointed experts, police and prosecutors have devised a new system under which child witnesses are questioned in specially constructed interview suites and the interviews are video recorded. The main aim is to enable the court of trial to see the interview for itself and thus discover exactly how the child was questioned. But the procedure has other advantages. A second investigator watches the interview from behind a one-way mirror, and

> in principle other officials can follow the interview behind the mirror too, for example the defence lawyer, psychologists or other experts. During the interview the questioner can even be advised from behind the mirror that a particular aspect needs to be given more attention. Thus the technical possibilities of an interview studio are great (Bonarius, 1994: 1167–71).

Finally, throughout continental Europe changes in criminal procedure allowing the defence a chance to put their questions to the witness are taking place under the influence of the European Convention on Human Rights. In most of these countries, unlike in Britain, this forms part of the law of the land. Article 6(3)(d) of this Convention guarantees for all defendants the right 'to examine or have examined witnesses against him'. In one important case, for example, the European Court of Human Rights upheld a complaint by a French defendant whom the French courts had convicted of robbing a 16 year-old girl in the Paris metro without the defence at any stage having the chance to put questions to the girl and her young friend (*Delta* v *France* (1993) 16 EHRR 574); and in France, the courts have taken account of this ruling. In the second part of this chapter we examine in detail what Article 6(3)(d) requires. For the moment, it is enough to say that Article 6(3)(d) requires the defence to be given an opportunity to put its questions to prosecution witnesses at some stage of the proceedings – although not necessarily at the trial.

Hearsay: the accusatorial systems

The notion of accusatorial justice, like the common law, grew up in England, and the countries with the most accusatorial systems are those whose laws derive from English law: besides England, these are the United States and the countries of the British Commonwealth. Accusatorial criminal justice systems of a basically accusational type are also found in other jurisdictions which, strictly speaking, are not part of the common law world. One is Scotland, and another is Israel. The Scandinavian countries also fall into this group, although the accusatorial tradition there is weaker. In the same position is Italy, which in 1988 enacted a new code of criminal procedure which borrows a number of ideas from the common law.

A prominent feature of the accusatorial systems is their strong preference for oral evidence. In most of these jurisdictions, this is expressed by either or both of the following two rules:

- *The rule against hearsay*. A party may not prove something happened by calling 'A', who did not see or hear or feel it, to testify that he heard 'B', who did, describe it; either 'B' must be produced to describe it orally to the court, or the incident must be proved by other means. (This rule, furthermore, extends to documents and tapes; 'A' is equally forbidden to produce a written statement from the absent 'B' describing the event, or even a video or audio tape of him describing it.)
- *The rule against narrative*. If 'B' does come to court to give oral evidence, the statements he previously made about the incident are suppressed – except where they contradict his oral evidence, in which case they can be used to undermine his credibility.

It may be that the common law systems originally insisted on oral evidence because cases were tried by juries, and jurors could not read. Whatever the origin of the rule, however, over the centuries the superiority of oral over written evidence eventually became an article of faith to common lawyers, and also became entwined in their minds with the need to allow the defendant in a criminal case to confront the person who accused him. These ideas, among others, underlie Article VI of the United States Bill of Rights – which provides, among other things, that the defendant in a criminal proceedings shall enjoy the right 'to be confronted with the witnesses against him'. In the USA this provision has been interpreted, in effect, as giving the defendant the right to 'eyeball' the witness when giving evidence at trial (*Coy* v *Iowa* (1988) 108 S Ct 2798; *Maryland* v *Craig* (1990) 1105 S Ct 3157).

As far as child witnesses are concerned, the insistence on oral evidence causes acute problems which are only too well known. The main way in which the accusatorial systems have tried to deal with this problem is by making the process of giving live evidence at trial less of an ordeal for child witnesses, in particular by the use of live television links to enable the child to testify live from outside the courtroom itself. But in most systems these techniques, if helpful for many children, have not proved on their own to be enough. Most of the accusatorial systems have therefore found it necessary to go further, and to create for children various exceptions to their normal rule that witnesses must give their evidence live by telling their story in person to the court of trial. These are of three broad types.

Admitting children's evidence as hearsay

In civil proceedings concerning children, the usual solution is to abrogate the hearsay rule completely, as was done in England in 1989 (Children Act 1989 s.96, Children (Admissibility of Hearsay) Order 1993). In criminal cases, the common law systems all recognise a number of exceptions to the hearsay rule which exceptionally enable the courts to hear what was said by certain absent witnesses, and the tendency seems to be for these exceptions to be expanded. In England, for example, the Criminal Justice Act 1988 now makes it possible, where the judge grants leave, for the court to hear the out-of-court statement of a witness who is too frightened to come to court. Obviously, these hearsay exceptions apply to the statements of children, as they do to those of adults. Some common law jurisdictions, like the State of Washington, for example, have even created new exceptions to the hearsay rule specifically to let in the statements of absent children in prosecutions for child abuse (Spencer and Flin, 1993: 136–7). In Canada, the Supreme Court produced a similar result by a ruling in a leading case (*Khan* v *R* (1991) 79 C.R (3d series) 1).

For the defendant in criminal proceedings, admitting the statement of an absent child under an exception to the hearsay rule has two serious disadvantages: first, it lets in statements which are potentially unreliable because there is no official control about how they were elicited or recorded, and secondly, it exposes him to conviction on the basis of an accusation by someone whom he has had no opportunity to confront or challenge. For this reason it might have been expected that the courts in the United States – which have invoked the defendant's constitutional protection under the Bill of Rights to limit the use that can be made of screens and other devices to make it easier for children to give live evidence – would have been particularly reluctant to allow defendants to be convicted solely on informal hearsay statements from absent children. Yet in 1992, a conviction so obtained was actually upheld by the Supreme Court of the United States (*White* v *Illinois*, US Supreme Court Reports (1992) 116 L Ed 2nd 848).

Admitting children's previous statements as an exception to the 'rule against narrative'

In many of the common law countries, a long-standing exception to the rule against narrative is 'recent complaint'. If someone who claims to be the victim of a sexual offence gives evidence at trial, the court may hear, to supplement the courtroom testimony, the terms of any complaint that person made, provided he or she complained spontaneously and at the earliest opportunity.

Over the last ten years, a number of common law jurisdictions have now created a new and potentially important exception to the rule against narrative involving videotapes. The previous statement of a child witness who testifies at trial is admitted, if video recorded. This development began in the United States, where the State of Montana enacted a law to this effect in 1977. Other jurisdictions in the United States followed, and so did Canada in 1987. In neither the USA nor Canada does this new exception to the rule against narrative seem to have been greatly used. Nevertheless, it was the change that the Home Office in England decided to promote when it rejected the proposals of the Pigot Committee, and Parliament enacted it in Part III of the Criminal Justice Act 1991, which sets up the legal framework for the arrangements that exist in England at present .

Providing for the whole of the child's evidence to be taken ahead of trial

Supplementing the child's courtroom evidence in this way gives the courts more evidence to work on. It does nothing, however, to improve the position of the child, who still has the stress of waiting to give evidence at trial, and of giving it having got there.

For this reason, some legal systems within the accusatorial tradition have gone further, and have introduced schemes which allow a child witness to be examined, with due formality, before a judge or other official person ahead of trial – the resulting formal record of the examination, or *deposition*, then replacing the appearance of the child as a live witness. In England, a law to enable this to be done in a case where appearing as a live witness at trial would involve serious danger to the child's life or health was enacted as long ago as 1894 – although this limited provision has been little used. In 1926, Norway introduced a scheme under which child witnesses in sex cases are examined, ahead of trial, by an examining magistrate (Andenaes, 1990). The Israeli scheme, under which a 'youth interrogator' is called in to question the child, and reports the child's answers to the court, is in principle the same – except that the person who takes the statement from the child is a person specially trained and designated (Harnon, 1988; 1990). These schemes, unlike the more limited English one, are widely used. In recent years, such an examination has been made possible in New Zealand (Evidence Act 1908 as amended, s.23E (1) (a) and (3)), in Scotland (Prisoners and Criminal Proceedings (Scotland) Act 1993 s.33), and in various jurisdictions in Australia. Statutes have also been passed to make this possible in a number of jurisdictions of the United States, although they seem to be little used there, mainly because of doubts about whether they are constitutional in the light of Article VI of the Bill of Rights. It was such a scheme as this, of course, that the Pigot Committee unsuccessfully proposed for England in 1989 (Home Office, 1989).

In principle, these schemes for pre-trial examination fall into two distinct types. In the first – as in Norway and Israel – a designated official examines the child on behalf of the court, without any input from the defence. The defence has some safeguard in the quality of the person who conducts the examination, and in Israel, the additional safeguard that he cannot be convicted on the basis of evidence so obtained unless there is corroboration, but it has no right to put questions to the child, or even to require the examiner to put them. In the second and more developed model, the defence are allowed to observe the examination, and given an opportunity to put their questions to the child. This is the scheme that evolved – in the absence of any precise legislative text – in Denmark (Andenaes, 1990), where defence counsel can watch the examination by closed-circuit television, and then put his questions to the child. The scheme enacted in Scotland in 1993 is also of this type, and so was the scheme devised by the Pigot Committee. In the older versions of such schemes the child's deposition is recorded in writing. In the more modern ones it is tape recorded, usually on videotape. This has the obvious advantage of enabling the court to know, beyond any possible doubt, just what was said: and for systems where the tradition favours evidence given orally, it also means that the court can actually see and hear the child.

In the broadest terms, it looks as if the inquisitorial and the accusatorial systems are converging on one aspect of the law relating to children's evidence. This is the necessity of providing, for at least some child witnesses, something on the lines of the Pigot scheme, under which all the child's evidence is taken ahead of trial, the defence are given at that stage a chance to put their questions, and the child thereafter takes no further part in the proceedings. In the inquisitorial systems, the pressure is the desire to provide the court with a fuller and more reliable account of what the child was saying, and to give the defence a chance to question the accuser; and in the accusatorial systems, the pressure is the need to enable the courts to receive the evidence of children who cannot cope with the ordeal of giving live evidence at trial.

Children's evidence and the European Convention on Human Rights

Although the European Convention is not directly applicable in the United Kingdom as it is in most of the rest of Europe, a breach of its terms can still result in proceedings being taken against the Government before the European Commission of Human Rights, and ultimately a condemnation by the European Court of Human Rights (ECHR). In practice, the Government usually tries to ensure that new legislation complies with the Convention.

When it comes to schemes to reform the ways in which children give evidence in criminal proceedings the most important provision of the Convention is Article 6. This Article provides in broad terms that defendants in criminal proceedings have a right to a fair trial, and then lists the features a trial must have to count as a fair one, one of which is the right for the defendant *'to examine or have examined witnesses against him'* (Article 6(3)(d)). The phrase 'witnesses against him' has been broadly interpreted. In a series of decisions the ECHR has ruled that a person counts as a prosecution witness – and hence as someone whom the defence has a right to question – not only where he or she is a witness in the usual English sense of a person who attends trial to give oral evidence, but also where he or she is someone who fed information into the criminal justice system at an earlier stage and which is later repeated to the court of trial by others (Law Commission, 1995). This means that Article 6(3)(d) renders potentially risky not only attempts to curtail the right of the defence to put their side of the case to children who testify live at trial, but also attempts to replace the child's live evidence at trial by something else: like hearsay statements made admissible under exceptions to the hearsay rule, or depositions, whether recorded in writing or on tape.

Three important questions arise as to the scope of Article 6(3)(d):

- Is the right to question a right to put questions to the witness orally at the trial, or is it enough for the defence to be given an opportunity to put their questions at an earlier stage in the proceedings?
- Is the right to question prosecution witnesses an absolute one? Or can

the prosecution sometimes use in evidence the statement of a witness whom the defence have been unable to question, provided that, all things being considered, the defendant still has a 'fair trial'?

● Does the right to question mean a right to put questions to the witness directly, or is it enough that the defence can put questions to the witness via a magistrate or judge?

Here is not the place for a detailed account of the case law of the ECHR 6(3)(d), but a recent case, *Doorson* v *The Netherlands* (1996) 22 EHRR 330, is worth examining because it involved a challenge to a scheme for the protection of vulnerable witnesses. Although the group in question were not children but witnesses who had been or were likely to be threatened, there are obvious analogies. The defendant, Doorson, had been convicted of selling drugs, and among the pieces of evidence upon which the Dutch trial and appeal courts convicted him were the statements of various people who claimed to be his customers. These witnesses consisted, first, of 'A'. He gave live evidence at trial, and under defence questioning retracted earlier statements to the police in which he had implicated the defendant; the Dutch courts, however, accepted his original statements as the truth and disbelieved his retraction. Then there were 'B' and 'C', who said they feared reprisals, and who under the Dutch law on threatened witnesses had been allowed to remain anonymous and had been questioned in private before a *rechter-commissaris*, their statements taken at this hearing being received as evidence by the court of trial, which did not hear them orally. At the hearing before the *rechter-commissaris* Doorson's lawyer was present and was allowed to ask them questions, but not Doorson himself. Lastly there was witness 'D', who fled after giving a statement to the police implicating the defendant, apparently in order to avoid any further questioning. The Dutch courts nevertheless treated as evidence his statement to the police. Before the ECHR, Doorson claimed that at trial his rights under Article 6 in general, and under 6(3)(d) in particular, had been denied him. His complaint failed, however, the ECHR concluding that overall his trial was fair.

With this case in mind, we can examine the three important questions about the scope of Article 6(3)(d) which were asked above.

To the first one, which is whether it suffices (as under the Pigot scheme) for the defence to have a chance to put their questions to a prosecution witness at an earlier stage in the proceedings than the trial, the answer is clearly 'yes'. This obviously follows from the *Doorson* case, where the Court approved of the way in which witnesses 'B' and 'C' had been examined (and where, incidentally, it also added that it it did not matter that the defendant himself was absent, given he was represented at the examinations by his advocate). It also follows from pronouncements in earlier decisions (in particular *Kostovski* v *The Netherlands* (1990) 12 EHRR 434).

To the second question, which is whether notwithstanding Article 6(3)(d) the prosecution can sometimes use in evidence the statement of a witness whom the defence have been unable to question, the answer once again is 'clearly yes'. In the *Doorson* case and a number of other recent cases, the ECHR has held that it is permissible to use as evidence the statement of witnesses whom the defence has been unable to question provided that the trial, taken as a whole, is fair; and in deciding whether the trial is fair or not, an important matter is whether these statements stand alone, or whether they are corroborated by other evidence. This has important implications for English law. First, it suggests that admitting children's statements under exceptions to the hearsay rule does not as such infringe the Convention. Secondly, it also suggests that the current rule of English law, under which – surprisingly – a piece of hearsay evidence admitted under some exception to the hearsay rule can form the basis for a conviction even if it stands alone, is contrary to the Convention (*Nembhard* v *R* [1981] 1 WLR 1515).

The third question, which is whether Article 6(3)(d) requires the defence to be allowed to put its questions directly, is also relevant to reforms about child witnesses. The Pigot Committee, it will be remembered, proposed to allow certain types of child witness to be examined non-adversarially, with a single neutral person putting to the child the questions of both prosecution and defence. Would such a scheme be contrary to Article 6(3)(d)? The ECHR has not so far answered this question, because nobody seems to have asked it. If asked whether Article 6(3)(d) is satisfied by a system under which the defence must put its questions to the witness indirectly, however, I believe that the ECHR would answer 'yes'. Although in the Common Law world we are used to witnesses being examined and cross-examined adversarially, in many parts of Europe (including France, Germany, Belgium and Holland) the usual practice is for all witnesses to be examined by the court, prosecution and defence being obliged to put their questions via the presiding judge, unless he or she allows them to put them to the witness direct. To many ECHR judges the suggestion that this sort of arrangement is contrary to the Convention would be astonishing.

Finally, before leaving the Convention it should be mentioned that defendants are not the only people who have rights under it. Victims and witnesses are not expressly protected by a provision like Article 6(3), but they share with other citizens the general guarantees offered by other Articles of the Convention, like Article 1 on the right to life, Article 5 on liberty and security of person, and Article 8 which guarantees respect for private life. In the *Doorson* case, the ECHR said that these rights had to be considered when interpreting the defendant's rights under Article 6. Not only this: they sometimes enable victims to take the offensive and attack the criminal procedure of their country by making a complaint to Strasbourg. In *X* v *The Netherlands*

((1985) Series A, No. 91), for example, the ECHR upheld a complaint by a mentally handicapped teenage girl that Dutch law did not adequately protect her private life because, in effect, it made it virtually impossible to prosecute a man who had sexually abused her. The offence in question was one which under Dutch law could only be prosecuted where the victim laid a formal accusation, and the girl was too seriously handicapped to be able to do this. In consequence of the ECHR ruling, Dutch law had to be changed.

From this brief discussion of the European Convention two things should be clear. The first is that the sort of scheme for protecting vulnerable witnesses that was devised by the Pigot Committee does not infringe the rights of the defendant under it. The second is that it is conceivable that the United Kingdom could some day find itself in trouble before the Commission and the Court at Strasbourg for failing to modify in favour of vulnerable witnesses a system which to some extent confers immunity on those who abuse them by making it too burdensome for them to give evidence (Law Commission, 1995: 70).

References

Andenaes, J. (1990), 'The Scandinavian countries', in J.R. Spencer, G. Nicholson, R. Flin and R. Bull (eds) *Children's Evidence in Legal Proceedings, an International Perspective*, Cambridge: Law Faculty, University of Cambridge.

Bonarius, J.C.J. (1994), 'Het horen van kinderen als getuige bij incest: het verschoningsrecht', *Nederlandse Juristen Blad*, 30, September, 1167.

Frehsee, D. (1990), 'Children's evidence within the German legal system', in J.R. Spencer, G. Nicholson, R. Flin and R. Bull (eds) *Children's Evidence in Legal Proceedings, an International Perspective*, Cambridge: Law Faculty, University of Cambridge.

Hamon, H. (1990), 'The testimony of the child victim of intra-familial sexual abuse', in J.R. Spencer, G. Nicholson, R. Flin and R. Bull (eds) *Children's Evidence in Legal Proceedings, an International Perspective*, Cambridge: Law Faculty, University of Cambridge.

Harnon, E. (1988), 'The examination of children in sexual offences – the Israeli law and practice', *Criminal Law Review*, 263–74.

Harnon, E. (1990), 'Children's evidence in the Israeli criminal justice system: with special reference to sexual offences', in J.R. Spencer, G. Nicholson, R. Flin and R. Bull (eds) *Children's Evidence in Legal Proceedings, an International Perspective*, Cambridge: Law Faculty, University of Cambridge.

Home Office (1989), *Report of the Advisory Committee on Video Evidence*, Chairman Judge Thomas Pigot QC, London: Home Office.

Law Commission (England) (1995), *Consultation Paper Evidence in Criminal Proceedings: Hearsay and Related Topics* (Law Commission Paper No. 138), Part V, London: HMSO.

McGough, L.S. (1994), *Child Witnesses: Fragile Voices in the American Legal System*, New Haven, CT: Yale University Press.

Pipe, M.-E. and Henaghan, M. (1996), 'Accommodating children's testimony: legal reforms in New Zealand', *Criminal Justice and Behaviour (Special Issue on Children's Testimony – International Perspectives)*, 23(2), 377–401.

Spencer, J.R. and Flin, R. (1993), *The Evidence of Children, the Law and the Psychology*, 2nd edn, London: Blackstone, ch. 14.

Spencer, J.R., Nicholson, G., Flin, R. and Bull, R. (eds) (1990), *Children's Evidence in Legal Proceedings, an International Perspective*. Papers from an international conference at Selwyn College, Cambridge: Law Faculty, University of Cambridge.

9 The investigation of organised abuse: considering alternatives

Liz Davies

The Memorandum of Good Practice on Video Recorded Interviews with Child Witnesses for Criminal Proceedings (Home Office, 1992a) is excellent guidance for the investigative interviewing of older children who wish to seek justice, have good verbal skills, the support of their carers and who are safe. These are not the children generally selected as victims of sexual and sadistic abuse by serial predatory paedophiles who systematically target the most vulnerable, isolated and rejected children. By placing the prime focus for conviction of offenders on children's evidence we pressurise children who already have suffered enough. With low conviction rates the existing system rarely achieves justice for children; and in criminal proceedings Section 1 of the Children Act 1989, which emphasises the paramountcy of the child's welfare, takes second place to the concept of a fair trial. Even when paedophiles have been convicted, the traumatic impact of the trial on children has led some professionals to recommend that, 'never again should child victims of sexual abuse have to undergo days of cross-examination by lawyers' (Dobson, 1994).

Organised abuse is perpetrated by adults against children and it is clearly adults who must seek to achieve justice for child victims (Davies and Higginson, 1995). A framework is required in organised abuse investigations which relies minimally on the need for children to be witnesses in criminal proceedings. A dual strategy is necessary to take the onus off children. This demands as one component the proactive, highly focused investigation of known and alleged perpetrators paralleled by broad spectrum intervention as the second component, aimed at creating an organised network of protective adults around children in the community.

In this chapter I propose to offer a practice based, alternative, adult focused approach to the investigation of organised abuse. I make reference to investigations in the London Borough of Islington because during the time of my employment in that Borough I worked to protect children from organised, institutional and ritual abuse. I subsequently gave evidence to the various inquiries and the Paedophile Squad at New Scotland Yard. I have since had the opportunity to develop practice skills in this fraught area of work, with the satisfaction of achieving positive outcomes for children.

I first make a plea for a change of attitude towards the child victims of this form of abuse and then go on to consider procedures to be used in the joint investigation of organised abuse, followed by an overview of community based, broad spectrum interventions which I argue must co-exist with the more sophisticated strategies. The *Memorandum*, as a precise method of interviewing child witnesses, finds its place as but one intervention within joint investigation procedures (see Figure 9.1).

Figure 9.1: An alternative approach to investigating organised abuse

Strand A: Highly focused, joint investigation/intervention

- Local/regional/national specialist multi-agency teams
- Identification of children at risk and strategies to protect
- Perpetrator focused strategies – surveillance, search of premises, scene of crime evidence, forensic retrieval
- Interviews with convicted paedophiles to seek intelligence about perpetrators and victims
- Collation of intelligence about perpetrators – mapping networks, methods, venues
- Intelligence gathering interviews
- Questionnaires given to alleged child victims as a filter before interviewing a select few
- Identification of adult witnesses
- Involvement of non-abusive carers/local community to assist the investigation
- *Memorandum* interviews – minimal involvement of children as witnesses in criminal proceedings

Strand B: Broad spectrum intervention

- Creating an organised network of protective adults in the community
- Training professionals and non-statutory workers in the early recognition of organised abuse
- Filtering information through the Area Child Protection Committee
- Self-protection work with children

The need for a change of perspective

Child victims of organised abuse are consistently failed by current multi-agency responses. Intervention is generally triggered by disclosures from children or reports to police child protection teams and social services. Both organisations primarily respond to intra-familial abuse and are not resourced to investigate perpetrators proactively. Organised abuse often comes to the attention of other agencies without triggering joint police/social services investigation. For instance, it is rare to attempt the identification of children from the vast numbers of child pornographic photographs and videos obtained following police searches of premises. Similarly, paedophiles may abuse hundreds of children in a lifetime and yet it is not usual to attempt to locate these victims. Using information about convicted paedophiles in East Sussex, Willis suggests a total of as many as 14,400 child victims in that area alone (Willis, 1993: 4).

The plight of missing children and lack of strategies to protect them was highlighted by Chief Superintendent Stoodley following the Operation Orchid investigation concerning abducted and murdered children in London and the South East. He commented, 'Children can vanish without trace, without anyone caring or looking for them. The bodies of young boys were being carried about the Kingsmead estate in broad daylight ... This gang based there has unquestionably killed more children than is known' (Oliver and Smith, 1993: 275). Wyre makes a similar point in his analysis of the child murderer Robert Black. 'If we can't protect our children 24 hours of every day, and we can't, we must work with offenders to reduce the risk that they will abduct, abuse or kill. There are thousands of men in Britain, at large and unnoticed, who are on the same path as Robert Black' (Wyre and Tate, 1995: 266). The insights gained by such professionals working with sex offenders must be incorporated within the investigative process if the numbers of children targeted are to have any chance of effective protection.

Numerous investigations of organised institutional abuse in boarding schools, residential care establishments and day care settings have increased knowledge about the recidivist nature of paedophilia and that offenders often change their identities and proceed to abuse children elsewhere. While there has been an essential emphasis on the need for improved vetting procedures (Home Office, 1992b; Coombes, 1995), there has been little central collation of intelligence or proactive investigation of the paedophiles involved. The tracking of such offenders often relies on an individual professional contacting the authority where they suspect a paedophile is working. Hughes and Parker (1994) argue that there should be a shift away from seeing child sexual abuse as a primarily social problem towards perceiving it as a serious crime. They are concerned that, 'there is no way of tracking perpetrators as they move around the country'. If legislation prevented Schedule One offenders changing their name by deed poll, and enforced registration of residence, it would be difficult for offenders to move the location of their offending (particularly abroad), and would provide information locally.

Strand A: joint investigation teams

Of foremost importance in the effective investigation of organised abuse is the establishment of local, regional and national joint investigation teams. Former Detective Superintendent of the Obscene Publications Squad, Michael Hames, has emphasised the urgent need for this development. 'The Police Child Protection Teams are doing a great job dealing with offences if they are reported. But that is not enough. We need a proactive, national squad to go out and gather information and target these people' (Davies, 1994). A very useful US analysis of such teams is offered by Spence and Wilson (1994: 13/14). They argue that, 'by working together, the team can accomplish the goals of all investigative agencies in a more efficient manner and with enhanced results'. In the UK, social workers used to working with the police child protection teams have to develop working relationships with officers from the CID and New Scotland Yard. These police officers need to become involved with joint investigation training and development. Joint work demands flexibility of role, and may, for example, involve social workers contributing their expertise to traditional police work such as scene of crime investigations and suspect interviews. The Home Office and the Department of Health would need to redirect existing resources to establish a central joint investigation team to take the lead in training and developing the regional teams.

The child abuse investigation in Islington provides a useful example of the importance of joint teams if children are to be protected from the activities of large scale paedophile rings. On 1 August 1993 a *Sunday Times* report stated that, 'Britain's biggest police inquiry into organised sexual abuse of children has been launched by Scotland Yard's Obscene Publications Squad'. It explained that the investigation had uncovered several groups across London and Southern England and included surveillance of some wealthy businessmen who had been linked to a sex ring abusing young children living in children's homes in the London Borough of Islington (Palmer, 1993).

Following extensive media coverage, 'The Report of the Inquiry into the Management of Local Authority Children's Homes in Islington 1995 (the 'White Report' – White and Hart, 1995), acknowledged that 61 children had been identified as possible victims of organised abuse in just one of the local offices. The police, however, had found no evidence of connections between individual children at risk from abuse and Scotland Yard had insufficient evidence for prosecutions. The Islington Area Child Protection Committee and the Social Services Inspectorate both concluded that there was 'no evidence to support the assertions of organised abuse' (White and Hart, 1995: 41–2).

This conclusion was flawed and betrayed the many child victims of paedophiles in that area of London. Although only one case led to conviction, the fact that there may have been insufficient evidence at that stage for further prosecutions did not prove that there was no organised sexual abuse of children (BASW, 1993). Professionals had profiled victims and offenders, and collated details of organised and ritual abuse which had led to civil proceedings, but in the absence of proactive collation of intelligence and multiagency planning across the 24 local offices and with neighbouring boroughs, it was impossible for the investigation to proceed to the higher level of proof required for the criminal courts. Without co-ordination with local multiagency teams the officers at Scotland Yard were limited in accessing intelligence and the locality professionals did not share the relevant knowledge held centrally by the Obscene Publications Squad. Without a central multiagency team, liaison proved difficult with a number of different social services departments, each with their own procedures and practices.

Methods of investigation

Collation of intelligence

When we examine the reasons why children rarely speak about their abuse by paedophiles, it is surprising that we place our investigative emphasis on children's disclosures. Threats from the paedophile, or from peers and family who do not want their own involvement in the ring exposed, may involve direct physical threats or the withdrawal of favours on which the child has come to depend, for example drugs, money, housing. Young people fear disbelief, particularly when the abuse is of a bizarre nature, and that disclosure – which rarely leads to conviction – may leave them more vulnerable. A paedophile's strategy will aim at the child's total emotional, physical and economic dependency on him or her and may well involve the child in the abuse of other children, child pornography or other criminal activities. The child will fear both his or her own and the paedophile's imprisonment and may well have to overcome this guilt and fear of punishment before feeling confident enough to disclose. A number of investigations have highlighted the involvement of respected members of the community in the abuse network, leading understandably to children's reluctance to disclose.

The main task of the joint investigation teams would be to find alternative methods of gaining evidence to protect children and to convict perpetrators. Collation of evidence of known and suspected offenders is the cornerstone of this work. A Register of Schedule One offenders is essential and would extend intelligence currently on file at the National Criminal Intelligence Service. Social services departments and the probation service are now informed by prison governors and consulted when Schedule One offenders are admitted to and released from custody (HM Prison Service, 1994). These notifications should be extended to include the police, and these agencies should also be alerted to information coming to the attention of mental health teams particularly concerning the release of sex offenders who had been admitted under Section 37 of the Mental Health Act (Buckley and Peterson, 1994). Joint investigation teams would use mapping techniques to examine networks between known offenders, their methods of targeting and abusing children and the venues used for their criminal activities.

Because very few paedophiles are convicted and the court system is so inadequate given the extent of the problem, it is imperative that information about suspected paedophiles form part of the team's database. The 'Report of the Social Services Inspectorate into the Case of Martin Huston' recommended, 'In situations where organisations or professionals have reason to believe that a person who has not been convicted of a relevant offence nevertheless presents a risk to children, the duty to protect children should override considerations for the right of the individual concerned' (DHSS, 1993: 152). While the principle is clear, there are procedures which can offer some degree of protection to adults who stand accused.

Multi-agency conferences could decide whether, on the balance of probabilities level of proof, abuse has occurred. This decision would be quite separate from any criminal proceedings. The Area Child Protection Committee would safeguard the information using a system similar to that of the Child Protection Register. The Area Child Protection Committee would organise an appeal procedure. Following such a conference decision, notification would be made as appropriate to the Department of Health Consultancy Service and the Department for Education List 99. The entry of a name on these lists would not depend, as at present, on disciplinary proceedings having taken place but on a multi-agency decision. The current requirement that the alleged abuser must be informed of these notifications would depend on the multi-agency assessment of whether such sharing of information would place any child at risk of significant harm.

It is accepted that children often disclose abuse gradually, and before continuing to disclose they commonly test the water of the professionals' response. Often the truth in a child's statement is overlooked as it appears implausible. Bizarre comments and clues can be systematically recorded and in time checked against known fact and placed in context.

Local information about offenders, such as press reports, would be added to the team's database and consideration would be given to interviews with convicted paedophiles for information about other victims and perpetrators. New evidence might lead the investigators to the identification of adult witnesses themselves abused as children, pre-empting the need for children to appear in court.

Of particular importance is information about missing children. An innovative survey of missing children notifications over a year conducted in Bedfordshire found that most referrals were simply recorded. The authors found a few children's circumstances particularly worrying, and concluded that 'it is only the hard core group that we would be interested in following up' (Shriane, 1995). These children were the most likely to be victims of paedophiles. John Fitzgerald of the Bridge Child Care Consultancy raised these issues following the West case: 'What happens when a child comes back from absconding? Who asks the question where they have been? Who decides whether to alert the duty officer in social services and if the child does not return, and what happens after the initial police search?' (Downey, 1995). An independent review into the case of one 12 year-old child in residential care in Islington commented that there had been a 'lack of urgency in responding to allegations that this young man was being abused or at risk' (White and Hart, 1995: 11). The boy had been missing 90 times and was alleged to have been the victim of paedophiles (Fairweather and Payne, 1994). Such children often acquire the label 'rent boy' or 'prostitute' and the adult perpetrators remain hidden from professional view.

Maps can be drawn locating the places missing children visit from a particular locality or children's home and may lead to the identification of venues used by paedophiles to create 'pools' of children available for abuse. Sometimes attempts can be made to trace a number of perpetrators from knowledge about the abuse of one child. It is known that paedophiles advertise their victims and market them. This premise can assist a team in the mapping process.

Child protection meetings – focusing on perpetrators

At child protection strategy meetings and conferences every minute detail of a child's life is debated as if it is public property. Descriptions of the child's anatomy, psychological history, feelings, thoughts and innermost secrets are discussed. In contrast, it is not unusual to hear little or nothing about the alleged perpetrator. Meetings could be convened to coordinate such information. The numbers of children at risk and the level of concern would be assessed and child protection plans made as necessary, including attempts to identify other child victims. This may involve surveillance or the search of premises. Child pornography or forensic material may be found which could lead to a conviction without the child having to be a witness or could add corroboration to a child's statement. Locating material may lead to the identification of more child victims and perpetrators.

Questionnaires

The scale of organised abuse investigations can seem overwhelming to professionals. In situations where a large number of children may be victims of abuse, thought might be given to the use of a questionnaire (see Appendix at end of chapter). Some investigators have conducted *Memorandum* interviews with 50–100 children concerning the activities of one alleged perpetrator without gaining enough evidence to press charges. Sometimes decisions to limit resources lead to valuable evidence being missed and children remain unprotected. A questionnaire offers an alternative and economical method of investigation in such situations. When it is not known how many children have been exposed to abuse, this method allows many children to be asked certain questions in a short space of time. From the responses it may be possible to identify children who are most likely to have been victims. The investigating team can then select a small group of children for *Memorandum* interviews. These would need to be held simultaneously to avoid contamination of evidence.

In one situation a holiday camp was the setting for a volunteer to indecently assault children. Numbers of children had attended the camp for short holidays. Following allegations made by two children, it was possible through use of the questionnaire to identify five additional child victims. The questionnaire and details of the conduct of the investigation were made available to the court. The evidence led to the conviction of the perpetrator.

Intelligence gathering interviews

It may be a decision of the team strategy meeting to conduct an intelligence gathering interview with a child. The purpose would be to seek information from the child which would assist the investigation of the alleged abuser/s. Questions might cover a description of the suspect's home, workplace or vehicle, knowledge of telephone numbers, methods used to target children, known associates, and so on. Ideally, information gained would lead to further investigation and the perpetrator being charged without the child having to give evidence. Children may feel empowered through this type of interview, through their knowledge that they had played an invaluable part in the investigation. There would be no pressure on the child to discuss any abuse to themselves and most importantly the child's identity would be protected so that they would feel as safe as possible from retaliation by the perpetrator. It would also be important to establish that the child would not alert the alleged abuser to the inquiries.

The interview should always be conducted in a relaxed manner preferably at a discreet location. The child must be assured of the absolute confidentiality of the interview and that they are not in any trouble. The lead interviewer should be someone known and trusted by the child – for example a teacher, carer/parent, residential social worker – in the presence of and guided by a social worker or police officer skilled in investigative interviewing. The approach to the child is clear: ' We would like you to help us in our enquiries about.' The rapport phase may not be as crucial as in a *Memorandum* interview, depending on the age and development of the child, but the general rules of investigative interviewing would apply.

If during the interview the child begins to disclose that they have been abused, that they are witness to the abuse of other children or that they have themselves abused, the interview must be terminated sensitively and the officer would explain to the child that a statement may be taken or a *Memorandum* or PACE interview conducted, unless it is already clear that the case will not lead to future proceedings. If the child is distressed they should have the choice about whether or not to continue the interview. When the interview is closed the child must be told about how they might be informed of any developments.

This type of interview presents no dilemma with regard to the child's need for therapy. In the research by Sharland et al. (1995) concerning professional intervention in child sexual abuse, they concluded that, 'rather alarmingly those affected by abuse that had occurred outside the close family received least help'. Intelligence gathering interviews, and the perpetrator-focused approach, minimise the need to rely on child witnesses and therefore children are free to access therapeutic help at the time when they need it, with no limitations on what may or may not be discussed.

Current trends in child protection – the difficulties in relation to organised abuse investigations

Partnership with parents and carers is a key principle of current child care practice and essential when the parent or carer is known to be non-abusive. The team would work closely with the non-abusive carer who would need a great deal of support in understanding the paedophile's grooming processes of both parent and child. Informed parents can often provide a key source of information and assistance to the team. However, if a parent is a Schedule One offender thought must be given as to whether it is in the best interests of the child to pursue such partnership. For instance, how does a child victim experience the abusive parent attending the case conference designed to protect the child? Willis (1993: 86) refers to the 'risk of empowering abusive parents' when pursuing the 'laudable aim' of 'working in partnership with parents'.

Some paedophiles are making use of Residence Orders under section 8 of the Children Act 1989, to gain parental responsibility of a child in uncontested cases when the the court does not routinely request a court welfare report. Local authorities can find themselves acting in partnership with such an abusive carer.

Other key concepts currently promoted within child protection work sit uncomfortably with the protection of children. Respecting the wishes and feelings of the child may not be straightforward when a child is entrapped by a paedophile. To allow a child who wishes to reside with a paedophile to do so may not be in the child's 'best interests'. Professionals have to act courageously to protect such children from manipulation by paedophiles which may involve hypnosis and other mind control techniques, quite apart from threats. Children are victimised for financial gain and are a valuable commodity for a paedophile. The abuser will strive to retain possession of the child he or she may have groomed for some time – even years.

Ghate and Spencer (1995: 17), suggest that abusive behaviour should only be defined as such when it is debilitating for a child, making a distinction between abusive action and the impact on the child. In the context of organised abuse this is inappropriate. A child victim in the early stages of grooming may be receiving treats and find the relationship enjoyable. Children previously deprived of affection may even 'thrive' on the attention they are receiving. These situations would demand intervention even though the child, unaware of the harmful effects of the abuse, is wishing the relationship to continue. There are many cases where children are desensitised to pain as a result of persistent abuse or would be very aware of the dire consequences to themselves of displaying any obvious impact of the abuse.

Farmer and Owen (1995: 35), emphasise the importance of avoiding an interventionist approach to child protection in less serious cases. They found that involving police early in investigations could be counter-productive. This approach has no place within organised abuse investigations. Social workers must work closely with the police from the outset where organised abuse is indicated even though concern for a particular child may be low level at that time.

Dawn raids have been the subject of much media criticism. Such actions might well be the best method of obtaining the required evidence in order to ensure the protection of many children without alerting the alleged suspect. Paedophiles network with each other with a high degree of sophistication and to some degree investigators find their own techniques and communication systems mirroring those of the perpetrators.

Strand B: broad spectrum intervention

Investigators can develop and create their own effective networks including channels of communication with the local community to ensure that the team does not become out of touch. To facilitate the relaying of information to the investigators, Area Child Protection Committee training and awareness raising must reach out to active community members, for example: school governors, tenants associations, charities, ethnic minority groups, neighbourhood watch, local political parties and churches. Such caring citizens can learn how to recognise the early signs of child sexual abuse and the importance of reporting their suspicions. Public meetings and constructive use of the media can encourage the establishment of an organised network of protective adults within the community. Relationships between the public and the professionals can become informed and trusted, based on discussion and actual contact rather than on media constructed fantasies.

Wyre is clear that paedophiles frequently seek out and gain jobs in child care agencies, 'once there they typically continue to abuse, and their new victims don't speak out' (Wyre and Tate, 1995: 229). There must be channels for the reporting of suspicion across agencies, a system of checks and balances. One professional in each agency could be the contact for staff from any agency to report concerns. This would provide a legitimate route for 'whistleblowers'. The designated professional would also be the channel for passing information to the team from within their agency.

Area Child Protection Committees should aim to create a culture of awareness of child sexual abuse within the authority in a similar way to the programmes that have trained staff countrywide in relation to equal opportunities and HIV/AIDS.

Finally, self-protection work with children themselves must continue to be taught within schools. This approach on its own places too great a responsibility on children, but it is an essential component when used in conjunction with the perpetrator-focused strategies described above. Children must have their own clearly trusted and understood channels for recognising and reporting abuse.

Conclusion

Robert Black said that 'short of locking the kids up' there was nothing the parents could have done to prevent his murder and abuse of children (Wyre and Tate, 1995: 226). It was beyond the means and knowledge of any parent to have stopped Black or any other serial paedophile. It was not beyond the means of professionals, employed to protect children, to have actively worked towards preventing such atrocities. In order to be effective these professionals must receive the full backing of civil servants and politicians. The protection of children from serial predatory paedophiles has to be firmly placed on the political agenda.

The *Memorandum* arrived in the wake of the events in the Orkneys. If the clock could be turned back, it would be interesting to know what would have happened if the children had been interviewed according to the guidance. If the actions of professionals and techniques of investigation had not been the focus of the inquiry (Clyde, 1992) would the inquiry have had the remit to consider whether or not the children had been abused? What if the focus had been on the alleged perpetrators as described in this chapter? The outcome for the children if that had been the case will never be known – that has to be left to informed speculation.

Acknowledgement

The author wishes to acknowledge PC Chris King, Harrow Police Child Protection Team, for his input on the questionnaires discussed in this chapter.

References

British Association of Social Workers (1993), *Submissions to the Independent Management Review into Aspects of Child Care in Islington*, July (confidential).

Buckley, N. and Peterson, H. (1994), 'Freed sex psychopath returns to terrorise his child victims', *Mail on Sunday*, 16 October.

Clyde, J. (1992), *The Report of the Inquiry into the Removal of Children from the Orkneys in February 1991*, Edinburgh, HMSO.

Coombes, R. (1995), 'Private screening', *Care Weekly*, 4 May.

Davies, L. and Higginson, S.(1995), 'Trial of the innocents', *Community Care*, 6–12 July, 22–3.

Davies, N. (1994), 'Red light for blue squad', *The Guardian*, 29 November.

Department of Health (1991), *Working Together: A Guide to Arrangements for Inter-agency Cooperation for the Protection of Children from Abuse*, London: HMSO.

Department of Health (1995), *Child Protection Messages from Research*, London: HMSO.

Department of Health and Social Security (DHSS) (1993), *An Abuse of Trust: The Report of the Social Services Inspectorate into the Case of Martin Huston*, London: HMSO.

Dobson, R. (1994), 'Children should be seen and heard', *Community Care*, 14–20 July, 14–15.

Downey, R. (1995), 'News special – protection for runaways sought', *Community Care*, 30 November, 5.

Fairweather, E. and Payne, S. (1994), 'Children abused by pimps in Islington', *Evening Standard*, 1 August.

Farmer, E. and Owen, M. (1995), *Child Protection Practice, Private Risks and Public Remedies*, London: HMSO.

Ghate, D. and Spencer, L. (1995), *The Prevalence of Child Sexual Abuse in Britain*, London: HMSO.

HM Prison Service (1994), *Guidance Notes Two: Instructions to Governors 54/1994 Release of Prisoners Convicted of Offences Against Children or Young Persons under the age of 18*, London: HMSO.

Home Office and Department of Health (1992a), *Memorandum of Good Practice on Video Recorded Interviews with Child Witnesses for Criminal Proceedings*, London: HMSO.

Home Office (1992b), *Choosing with Care: Report of the Committee of Inquiry into the Selection, Development and Management of Staff in Children's Homes* (The Warner Report), London: HMSO.

Hughes, B. and Parker, H. (1994), 'Save the children', *Community Care*, 3 March, 24–5.

Oliver, T. and Smith, R. (1993), *Lambs to the Slaughter*, London: Warner Books.

Palmer, R. (1993), 'Child abuse sex ring found', *The Sunday Times*, 1 August.

Sharland, E., Jones, D., Aldgate J., Seal, H. and Croucher, M. (1995), 'Professional intervention in child sexual abuse', in Department of Health, *Child Protection Messages from Research*, London: HMSO, 79.

Shriane, H. (1995), *Luton Runaways: The Profile*, Luton: NSPCC.

Spence, D. and Wilson, C. (1994), *Team Investigation of Child Sexual Abuse*, London: Sage.

White, I. and Hart, K. (1995), *Report of the Inquiry into the Management of Local Authority Children's Homes in Islington*, London: London Borough of Islington.

Willis, G. (1993), *Unspeakable Crimes*, London: The Children's Society.

Wyre, R. and Tate, T. (1995), *The Murder of Childhood*, Harmondsworth: Penguin Books.

APPENDIX: The use of questionnaires in organised abuse investigations

1   *When to use a questionnaire*

It is not always appropriate to use a questionnaire. This method provides a way of interviewing a large number of children in a short space of time, where it is not known how many children have been exposed to abuse. A questionnaire is used to identify potential victims and witnesses, and to gather coherent information about the club/group/holiday regime from the child's perspective.

2   *Who should decide whether or not a questionnaire is to be used in a particular investigation?*

The decision should be made at a joint strategy meeting with legal services present. If the Crown Prosecution Service are involved, they should also be consulted.

3   *Writing the questionnaire*

The questionnaire must be worded age appropriately. Its questions must be clear, non-leading and deliberately non-specific about the abuse, and there must be space for young people to add their own comments. The questionnaire might contain the caution that the child completing it must not discuss what they have written with anyone else. It may be necessary to produce the questionnaire in a number of languages.

4   *Making the questionnaire relevant*

Questions should relate to the particular inquiry, and it might be necessary to ask specific questions, e.g. 'Where did you sleep?' or 'Who sat next to you on the bus?' The details of the abuse must be kept from the children and they should have the opportunity to tell about abuse without any kind of prompting.

5   *Preparing the parents/carers*

Depending on the situation, a meeting of parents may be called or a letter sent to ask for their cooperation. Consideration needs to be given to contamination of evidence through parents discussing the matter together. If some young people have already disclosed, then there must be planning to ensure that those families are not identifiable,. e.g. agree with those parents that their children also get a letter to take home even though they do not need to complete the questionnaire. Contact with parents must be ethnically and culturally sensitive, and thought must be given to the needs of parents and carers who are non-literate. Contact numbers must be provided should they have any queries or concerns.

6   Preparing the young people

A letter may be worded to the young people but obviously without conveying any detail of known allegations. They should be informed that the questionnaire is confidential and will only be shared with the investigating team. If some young people have already disclosed, their identities must be protected both to ensure their safety and to prevent contamination of evidence. In the usual situation these children would not be completing a questionnaire but the above would apply where the questionnaire is distributed in a classroom. Children should be given the name of a member of staff or a member of the investigating team to whom they can talk.

7   Preparing the staff

It might be considered in the best interests of the children to distribute the questionnaire in familiar surroundings for them, e.g. a classroom. The staff must then be prepared to present the information correctly and the investigating team should be available in case any young person wishes to talk with someone during or following the completion of the questionnaire. Staff will need support throughout the whole exercise and for the days following as issues arise.

8   Evaluating the response

The questionnaire should be collated immediately and parents contacted as soon as it is practicable to inform them of any concerns. If the questionnaires have been completed at home it is important that the parents have feedback quickly. When the questionnaires are collated, a strategy meeting should be convened and decisions made about whether or not to interview any of the young people and to prioritise the interviews. Staff who have an understanding of the young people may assist in the evaluation process. It is not unusual for the scope of the investigation to be widened following the analysis of the questionnaires, and consideration must also be given to any young people who did not complete the form.

Sample questionnaire

This is an example of a questionnaire which is based on an investigation where an allegation of abuse has been made about a leader at a youth club. The young people would be about 12 years old.

Child's name ....

1   Are you a member of .... club?

2   How long have you been a member of .... club?

3   If you have left the club, why did you leave?

4   What activities do you enjoy most at the club?

5   Why do you like these activities best?

6   Which activities don't you like?

7   Why don't you like these activities?

8   What are the names of the youth leaders at the club?

9   Is there a youth leader you

   a) like?   who?   why?
   b) dislike?   who?   why?

10   Has anything happened at the club that you did not like? Yes/No

11   If Yes – what was it you did not like and why?

12   Have you ever been worried or frightened by anything at the club? Yes/No

13   If Yes – what was it that worried or frightened you?

14   Have any of your friends told you that they have been worried or frightened?

15   Is there anything else you would like to say?

Signed ....

Date ....

10 Next steps after the *Memorandum*: preparing children for court

Jan Aldridge

In the 1950s the Robertsons made a powerful film of a 2 year-old going to hospital for the removal of her tonsils (Robertson, 1970). This film high-lighted the common ritualised procedures of the time, the lack of preparation and the lack of support. It also monitored the distress of the child and her sense of bewilderment and helplessness. Since that time there have been many changes in our society. We now recognise the vital importance of preparation and support in helping children cope effectively with special and potentially traumatic events in their lives, such as hospitalisation or starting school. This idea has arrived late, however, in the legal arena. As more and younger children come to court the adult-oriented legal system is beginning to be aware of its difficulties in serving the child citizens of our society as well as the adult ones. Despite this growing awareness, cultural attitudes and traditional systems can be slow to change.

Historically, the criminal law has pronounced a bias against children as credible witnesses. Even today the legal system's distrust of the credibility of the child witness remains pervasive, despite the consistent findings of a large body of psychological research which shows that even young children have considerable cognitive skills and abilities, that they can be reliable witnesses and that they are no more likely to lie than adults (Burton, 1976; Goodman, 1984; Spencer and Flin, 1993).

Major recommendations for change have been made in the last 10 years (for example the Pigot Committee's *Report of the Home Office Advisory Group on Video Evidence* (Home Office, 1989)), but until such time as these are fully implemented it seems likely that the majority of children will have to con-tinue to offer some, if not all, of their evidence in court. In this context it is important to consider how best children might be prepared for their encounter with the legal system. Most of the literature on the subject focuses on the criminal setting as this is the context in which they are most frequently called as witnesses. Further, it is the most adversarial setting in which a child may appear. The system is designed to guarantee the defendant's rights and not to provide safety and comfort for the child. It is only relatively recently that systematic attempts have begun to look at the issue of safeguarding children's well-being and preparing them for participation in the legal process.

In this chapter the main phases of stress for the child witness are first discussed and children's lack of knowledge of the court system described. Ways of preparing children are then considered that address both the enhancement of their capacity to give evidence and their anxiety about the process of doing so.

Sources of stress

Spencer and Flin (1993) describe three distinct phases of stress for the child witness:

- the experience of the crime itself
- the pre-trial period
- the trial itself.

Each of these phases will be considered in turn.

The experience of the crime

While this is not stress caused by the legal process its impact must be acknowledged and, particularly in the case of children who have been abused, its effects upon the children clearly understood. Children who have been abused are often fearful and anxious and can frequently be uncommunicative and withdrawn or overly compliant in strange and unfamiliar situations. The implications for such a child taking part in legal proceedings are worryingly clear (see Chapter 5).

The pre-trial period

Uncertainty about the length of this period can be a major cause of stress, as can the repeated delaying and re-scheduling of court dates. It is now government policy to give priority to child abuse prosecutions but in fact recent research has found that such cases are actually taking longer than the national average criminal case (Plotnikoff and Woolfson, 1995). In the United Kingdom it is the usual procedure in cases of intra-familial abuse for the child, rather than the alleged adult perpetrator, to be removed from the home. This means that the victim of the abuse may be coping with the loss of family members during this period, as well as dealing with possible retaliation from the family for the consequences of their action.

During this pre-trial waiting period a further major cause of stress is the fear of the unknown brought about by the lack of knowledge most children have of the legal system. Researchers and clinicians in Scotland, Australia, North America and the United Kingdom have examined how children perceive the legal system, what they know about court and how the prospect of going to court makes them feel (Feber, 1985; Goodman and Reed, 1988; Flin et al., 1989; Saywitz, 1989; Dezwirek-Sas, 1992; Freshwater and Aldridge, 1994). Children have consistently been found to have only limited knowledge of what will happen in court, the roles of the various professionals, and the role of the witness. Flin et al. (1989) interviewed school children (aged 6, 8 and 10 years) and found a very limited comprehension of legal vocabulary and proceedings. Of particular concern was the fact that children often said that they knew the meaning of a particular term but in fact did not understand it accurately. Freshwater and Aldridge (1994) interviewed child witnesses, school children and adults about their knowledge of court. They also found that children and young people have significant misunderstandings about the legal system. Surprisingly, child witnesses with their greater involvement with the legal system did not know more than uninvolved school children. This is in line with the findings of Saywitz (1989), that prior experience with the legal system did not lead to enhanced knowledge or understanding of the process. As children grow older their understanding of certain terms and concepts increases but they continue to misunderstand others. This partial understanding can obviously cause considerable problems in court. Common misunderstandings are that the victim is also the defendant and in some way also on trial, and that the prosecutor is someone who punishes you. The misunderstandings found among some of the adults in the same study by Freshwater and Aldridge (1994), are consistent with the findings over a number of years of widespread ignorance on the part of the adult public about legal matters (Banks et al., 1975). As well as preparing the child, witness programmes also need to address the issue of properly informing the parent or carer who may be supporting and reinforcing the work with the child.

A further cause of stress during the pre-trial period is the way in which information is gathered from the child for the decision-making process - a process about which children are not always consistently and reliably informed. Once a child has told or begun to tell people about what happened an interview is arranged in line with the *Memorandum of Good Practice on Video Recorded Interviews with Child Witnesses for Criminal Proceedings* (Home Office, 1992). Research on children's experiences of this procedure is scarce but what evidence is available suggests that children are not always clearly and consistently informed in an age-appropriate manner about the role, style and purpose of such interviews (Chapters 4 and 5).

The trial itself

The third phase identified by Spencer and Flin (1993) is the trial itself. Many months after the event the child is called to give evidence in an alien and frightening environment. On arrival in court there is often a considerable wait and this may be in the same place as others involved in the trial, including the defendant or the defendant's supporters. The layout of the court may be daunting, particularly in large courts where the acoustics are poor and the witness box relatively isolated from the rest of the court. This can heighten the child's feelings that they themselves are on trial. There may be a large audience and where the judge has not exercised the right to exclude the public this may include antagonistic supporters of the defendant. The fundamental principles of criminal law are designed to guarantee freedom and justice in our society, and to protect the rights of the accused. Child witnesses often feel the system is stacked against them and the credibility of their statements. Harvey (1991: 252) noted that children often express 'quizzical confusion' about a number of aspects of the legal system. For instance, 'Why does the accused have the right to remain silent?' In other words, 'Why do the victims have to go through all the rigours of investigation and trial as if they are not believed, when it appears the accused does not have to say anything?'

The formality, use of legal jargon and questioning tactics of the defence during cross-examination can be particularly confusing, especially as children may not understand the purpose, or even the wording of such questions. Children's definitions and misunderstandings of cross-examination are wide and varied ranging from 'they are examined by medical people, like with a rape victim' (male 14 years) to 'the court trial is done again if the judge can't decided if he is guilty or not' (female 15 years) (Freshwater and Aldridge, 1994). Despite this lack of understanding of cross-examination the child must go through the experience of having their capacity to recall accurately challenged by a defence counsel whose job it is to test their evidence and who may choose to interpret this as meaning by whatever means available. If the defence cannot discredit the evidence, a questionable but common strategy is to attempt to discredit the person; a disconcerting strategy for experienced adult witnesses, but particularly confusing for children.

In addition to the three phases of stress identified by Spencer and Flin (1993) it is becoming increasingly apparent that it is also important to consider what happens *post-trial*. This is a potentially important fourth phase of stress for many children and their families (Aldridge and Freshwater, 1993). After giving evidence many witnesses have no further contact with the legal system, indeed there are often no formal mechanisms to inform them even of the outcome of the trial. Where a child has been a central witness there is often a need for a significant debriefing, to help them make sense of their experiences and to integrate them into the wider context of their lives. This was found to be one of the parts of a preparation programme that the children themselves valued the most (Aldridge and Freshwater, 1993). The exact nature and extent of this debriefing will be dependent upon the individual child and the resources of the family, but it is important that the need for it is at least considered.

Preparation of child witnesses for court

The Royal Commission on Criminal Justice has recognised the importance of victims and other witnesses being 'given the support and encouragement that many need' (rc 196) and being protected from intimidatory questioning through the intervention of the judge. In North America, Canada and the United Kingdom programmes of preparation are being developed and evaluated, and found to be effective in terms of education, stress reduction, increased self-esteem, and improved ability to testify (Deswirek-Sas, 1992; Sisterman-Keeney, et al., Mellor and Dent, 1994). In addition, the programmes are being well received by children and their carers (Aldridge and Freshwater, 1993). However, despite individual initiatives systematic, structured preparation programmes that are integrated into the wider system and owned by the legal system are still relatively rare. This is unfortunate as it would be one way to address the anxiety that preparation and coaching might be confused, as well as concerns that preparation might contaminate a child's evidence. This anxiety appears to have its origins in anecdotal accounts of adults' and adult defendants' experiences of the legal system, particularly in dubious accounts of how defendants may be rehearsed or 'taken through their evidence' by their lawyers. There are few systematic preparation programmes for adults and few enforceable guidelines on what is and is not acceptable preparation for their involvement in the legal process. However, the child preparation programmes that are being developed clearly emphasise that their purpose is to prepare children for their encounter with the legal system, and so enable them to put their evidence before the court as fully and accurately as possible. They are unfailingly clear that preparation does not mean rehearsing or coaching children in terms of their individual testimony.

An important initiative in the United Kingdom in terms of the availability of government endorsed preparation materials is the *Child Witness Pack* (NSPCC/ChildLine, 1993) and the complementary training and resource guide 'Preparing Child Witnesses for Court' (NSPCC/ChildLine, 1994). The purpose of the guide is to assist trainers to provide training for those involved in preparing and supporting child witnesses. Preparing and supporting child witnesses is defined in the guide (NSPCC/ChildLine, 1994: 8) as:

- Assessing the child's needs in relation to a court appearance and planning how these needs can best be addressed.
- Direct work with the child to help them understand the court procedures and answer their questions and address their feelings and generally prepare them.
- Conveying relevant information to key professionals, such as police, the Crown Prosecution Service and court staff.
- Working with key figures in the child's life who have a role to play in relation to support and preparation, such as parents and carers.
- Providing an opportunity for discussion and support after the hearing and if necessary for follow-up work.
- Identifying additional and specialist sources of help for vulnerable children.

Despite this encouraging work, Plotnikoff and Woolfson (1995) found that a significant proportion of child witnesses in the criminal justice system do not even receive a copy of the *Child Witness Pack*. Further, they found that in cases where adults were working with the pack preparing children few had received any specific training. Davies et al. (1995) reported that 30 per cent of the child witnesses in their study had no preparation for court. Mellor and Dent (1994), reviewing the research relating to the preparation of witnesses in England and Wales, conclude that few children ever receive systematic and planned preparation for their appearance in court. In terms of less structured programmes there have, however, been some encouraging developments. Each Crown Court centre has appointed a child liaison officer whose job it is to promote the welfare of child witnesses when in contact with the Crown court and to provide a focal point for liaison with other agencies.

Key components of preparation programmes

Although research in the area of preparation of child witnesses is in its infancy there is a considerable degree of practical agreement emerging from the existing preparation programmes cited in the literature on the potentially important components to include (for example, Saywitz, 1989; Harvey, 1991; Deswirek-Sas, 1992; Sisterman-Keeney, et al., 1992; Aldridge and Freshwater, 1993). These components can be grouped into seven key areas which entwined together form the basis for a sound preparation programme which might then be adjusted to the specific needs of the individual children. These seven areas are:

- Assessment
- Education

- The giving of testimony
- Enhancing emotional resilience
- Involving the child's carer(s)
- Liaison and practical arrangements
- Debriefing.

Assessment

Children's many fears about going to court do not decrease with age (Freshwater and Aldridge, 1994). It is important to be aware of each specific child's level of anxiety and fear related to testifying, of the availability of family support and to have some appreciation of how they are functioning in a wider developmental context, particularly in terms of language and cognitive skills, and social and emotional development. In order to be in a position to do this effectively the adult needs a considerable understanding of developmental issues – or at least a readiness to learn.

Education and information giving

The value of providing children with information which enables them to understand the issues and procedures involved in a criminal trial was recognised by the Lord Chancellor when he spoke at the launch of *The Child Witness Pack* in 1993 (NSPCC/ChildLine, 1993). Exactly how children have been helped to understand the basic principles of the criminal justice system, their role in it, the functions and responsibilities of the personnel and the procedures of the courtroom varies from study to study and with local facilities and arrangements. Techniques include drawing, colouring books, photographs, videos, courtroom models, role plays in mock courts, visits to courts, role plays in real courts. The list is limited only by the workers' imaginations. Informal feedback from children is that they appreciate a range of approaches but they particularly value the inclusion of two aspects:

- An opportunity to visit the actual court-house at least once, and if possible more than once.
- A meeting with the prosecution, helped by having previously kept a 'book of questions' in which they have been encouraged to write down any queries for the prosecutor.

A related and important issue is the opportunity for the individual child to express their wishes about how they would like to give their evidence. Only when the child or young person really knows what is involved in appearing in open court, or in giving their evidence via a 'live-link' or by a pre-recorded videotaped interview possibly replacing their evidence-in-chief, can they be part of an informed decision-making process. In Cashmore's (1990) important study of Australian children's experiences of giving evidence it was not so much the means by which the children gave evidence that was important, but more the opportunity to be genuinely involved in making an informed choice.

The giving of testimony

Children in England and Wales may well be testifying more than one year after the incident about events that evoke fear, confusion and misunderstanding. Many of the adult participants are ignorant of child development issues and the dynamics of abuse. Alternatively they may feel that the fundamental principles of criminal law supersede any considerations for the child. Once the child's evidence-in-chief has been received, either in person or via the pre-recorded video, the cross-examination by the defence begins. While the tactics of cross-examination may be viewed as a method of testing the honesty of articulate adults, as a best way of testing the evidence of a child they leave a lot to be desired. In practice, cross-examination can serve as a technique to confuse and intimidate the child (Harvey, 1991; Westcott, 1995). Although there are many avenues to challenge the child's allegations the cross-examination of the child is typically an important focus. The aim of cross-examination is definitely not to have an opposing witness give a clear, complete and convincing account of the alleged incident(s). As Yuille (quoted in Harvey, 1991) has noted,

> One only needs to witness a single instance of the cross-examination of a child witness to realise that the procedure is ill suited to children. It is easy to confuse a young child with the use of age-inappropriate language, long and circuitous questions, and a confrontational style. The adversarial system creates as many problems as it solves in the area of child sexual abuse.

In the present climate of concern regarding the interview techniques used to take statements from child victims (Butler et al., 1991) more attention should be paid to the questioning techniques being used in the courtroom to test children's evidence (Cashmore, 1991). The Irish Law Commission stated in its 1989 Consultation Paper on Child Sexual Abuse,

> The lawyer needs to be able to understand the language of children and to be able to communicate with children, not in the esoteric language of the law, but in language appropriate to the particular stage of the child's development (p. 195).

Despite these concerns and serious reservations at the present time there is no alternative. How best then may children be prepared? Flin and Spencer (1995) suggest that there are at least five critical competencies for a child witness in court that may be improved by a pre-trial preparation pro-gramme. They suggest the child should be able to:

- recall information completely and accurately
- understand the lawyer's questions and, if necessary, indicate non-comprehension
- resist complying with leading questions
- cope with feelings of anxiety
- understand the trial process.

The first three of these are directly relevant to the giving of testimony and will be addressed in turn.

Recall information completely and accurately

Unfortunately, completeness and accuracy do not sit well together in children's testimony (Dent, 1992). 'Free narrative' descriptions are often accurate but incomplete. If more information is sought via questions completeness improves but at the expense of accuracy. It is, however, possible to help children learn to provide the greater information expected in a forensic context. Examples include, teaching children narrative elaboration and the use of self-cueing of 'wh' (who, what, where) questions (Saywitz, 1995); and context reinstatement (Wilkinson, 1988).

Understand the questions and indicate non-comprehension

In everyday life children will attempt to make sense of questions that are put to them, even apparently unintelligible ones, and answer at least a part of them. In preparing children for answering questions in court they need to be taught to listen carefully, to identify the questions (or part of the question) that they do not understand and to ask for the question to be re-phrased. The importance should be stressed of erring on the side of seeking clarification if they are unsure about what is being asked, rather than guessing as they are encouraged to do in school.

Resist complying with leading questions

When a child knows the answer to a question is different from the one being suggested they may still comply with the adult if it is put in the form of a leading question. This does not mean the child thinks the adult is right, it just means that they are complying. Children do this for a number of reasons, including being afraid to disagree, assuming adults know something more, and a desire to please. In the court context children need to learn not to do this. They need to understand that it is the adult's job to make certain the child is sure and that one way of doing this is to suggest things were different from the way the child said or to put guesses into the form of questions. In this context children need explicit permission to behave differently from what many perceive as the correct social norm. For example, being appropriately assertive and even contradicting the adult if they are incorrect with 'No, that is wrong' or 'It wasn't like that'.

Enhancing emotional resilience

Included in almost all of the more comprehensive preparation programmes are elements of stress reduction and anxiety management training to help the children address their fears, reduce their anxiety and engender a sense of self-empowerment. These usually draw on a number of psychological techniques, including aspects of relaxation training (Koeppen, 1974; Bernstien and Borkovec, 1973; Snaith et al., 1992), systematic desensitisation and guided imagery, breathing exercises and cognitive restructuring and empowerment, including positive self-statements of mastery and strength (Kendell, et al., 1988). There are many useful texts for those wishing to explore work in this area but a possible place to begin is Varma's edited book, *Anxiety in Children* (1984).

The involvement of the child's carer(s)

If carers are involved in the process of preparation then both carer and child can develop an understanding of the court system and know what to expect (Plotnikoff, 1990b). In practice carers are rarely involved in preparation. In some cases this is because the young person may prefer them not to be involved (Mellor, 1991). However, unless parallel provision is made, there is a danger that the adult's continuing misunderstandings and apprehension are communicated to the child and the benefits of preparation reduced. In addition, the child may feel the burden of supporting their carer at this difficult time, rather than the other way round.

Liaison and practical arrangements

Children's needs within the court should be communicated prior to the court date (Plotnikoff, 1990b). As noted earlier, children are rarely given the chance to express an informed opinion on how they would like their evidence to be heard. It is important that children are consulted when arrangements are being made for them. There are a range of options for taking children's evidence, but since there is no automatic right to these special facilities it is necessary to make formal requests in advance and to follow these up until a decision is made. Lines of communication are not always clear (Plotnikoff and Woolfson, 1995). Procedures are needed for making these decisions in advance of the trial wherever possible rather than 'on the day' and require the cooperation of the police, social services, the Crown Prosecution Service, crown court child liaison officer and judges. Separate waiting facilities for the child must also be considered, away from the defendant or defendant's relations as many children find it very intimidating to wait in the same room.

Despite the consistent research findings that children value the opportunity to meet the prosecution barrister before the hearing, and despite clear indications that it is beneficial, in practice child witnesses are rarely given the opportunity to do so (Report of Home Office Advisory Group, 1989; Plotnikoff, 1990b). Some barristers resist this suggestion on the grounds of custom and practice. The Code of Conduct (*Blackstone's Criminal Practice*, 1992) for the bar prohibits discussion of a case with a witness whom counsel may expect to examine, but it does not prohibit barrister and child witness meetings for the purpose of 'breaking the ice'. When barristers are prepared to meet the child it is one of the aspects of preparation programmes that is consistently appreciated by the children.

Another matter that is helpful to decide in advance is the question of support for the child in court. Children can benefit from having a familiar, trusted person present while they are giving their evidence (Plotnikoff, 1990a). There is ongoing debate as to who is an acceptable support person to both the child and the court. Courts can be quite rigid in this matter and not infrequently a support person can be excluded at the last moment in favour of an unfamiliar court usher (Mellor and Dent, 1994). This can be quite traumatic for some children as 'kindly' does not necessarily equate with 'supportive' to the child.

A final task in the area of liaison is to feed back problems with a view to subsequent modification of practice. In an area where time pressures are great and work loads high this task can be overlooked. It is, however, essential in the development of a good service. This is explicitly emphasised in 'Preparing Child Witnesses for Court' (NSPCC/ChildLine, 1994): 'A key element of a quality service is the opportunity to feedback problems to relevant bodies, for example, Area Child Protection Committee, Area Criminal Justice Liaison Committee, Courts Users Group.'

Debriefing

In the opinion of the children themselves the follow-up and debriefing post-trial can be one of the most important parts of a preparation programme (Aldridge and Freshwater, 1993). A number of questions need to be addressed in this period. How is the child? What are their fears, concerns and disappointments? What effect has the trial and outcome had on the child's self-esteem? What are the plans for the future? The child and family may need varying degrees of support to help them come to terms with and make sense of the court verdict. Should referral to another agency be considered? Do claims need to be instigated on the child's behalf to the Criminal Injuries Compensation Board? This follow-up period is also a time for the child's efforts to be acknowledged. Harvey (1991) recommended the use of an acknowledgement letter or symbol, or certificate of participation.

Unresolved issues

Exactly how preparation should be offered and by whom is unclear. Provision is variable, with implementation ranging from patchy to non-existent. Choices and controversies remain to be addressed. These include such questions as whether there should be preparation in a group or individual format; standardised or individualised programmes; and what agency or group of professionals might take responsibility for assisting child witnesses and what are their training needs. Further work is clearly needed to determine the most effective components of preparation programmes, to address individual differences and needs, including different needs linked with gender, disability, culture and ethnic group, as well as developmental stage, and to help decide which components are most suited to which children.

Conclusion

In the past the legal hurdles placed in the way of children giving evidence in criminal trials have been formidable (Davies and Drinkwater, 1988). As a society we are now questioning our assumptions that our youngest members are always the least able witnesses or the ones who can provide the least. In recent years there have been major changes in the laws governing children's evidence, particularly in terms of the actual process of giving evidence and courtroom modifications. There is much ongoing heated debate about how much further we still have to go if children are to have access to justice but there is growing agreement that children require 'more than a nod towards child-centred considerations' Spicer (1994: 159). As Barbara Joel-Esam (1994: 231), a lawyer with the National Society for the Protection of Cruelty to Children has put it,

> The balance of fairness at present is heavily weighted against the more vulnerable child witnesses ... The court system ... demands that children mould themselves to accommodate the requirements of the court process. If a vulnerable child

witness cannot meet these requirements they are either excluded from the court process or they suffer from being put through the trauma of that process.

It is important that the debate on major reforms continue, while meantime alongside it we help children cope with the legal system as it exists at present.

References

Aldridge, J. and Freshwater, K. (1993), 'The preparation of child witnesses', *Tolley's Journal of Child Law*, 5(1), 25–8.

Amacher, E. (1989), 'Group preparation of children for court: an idea whose time has come', *Roundtable Magazine*, 1(2), 14–17.

Banks, C., Malloney, E. and Willcok, H. (1975), 'Public attitudes to crime and the penal system', *British Journal of Criminology*, 15, 228–40.

Bernstein, D.A. and Borkovec, T.D. (1993), *Progressive Relaxation Training: A manual for the helping professionals*, Campaign: Research Press.

Blackstone's Criminal Practice (1992), Appendix 2, Part VI, 'Conduct of work barristers', London: Blackstone Press, 2124.

Burton, R. (1976), 'Honesty and dishonesty', in T. Lickona (ed.) *Moral Development and Behaviour*, New York: Holt, Rhinehart and Winston.

Butler, J., Glasgow, D. and McEnery, A. (1991), 'Child testimony: the potential of forensic linguistics and computational analysis for assessing the credibility of evidence', *Family Law*, 21, 34–7.

Cashmore, J. (1990), 'The use of video-technology for child witnesses', *Monash Law Review*, September, 16, 228–250.

Cashmore, J. (1991), 'Problems and solutions in lawyer-child communication', *Criminal Law Journal*, 15, 193–202.

Davies, G., Wilson, J.C., Mitchell, R. and Milsom, J. (1995), *Videotaping Children's Evidence: An Evaluation*, London: HMSO.

Dent, H. (1992), 'The effects of age and intelligence on eye-witnessing ability', in H. Dent and R. Flin (eds) *Children as Witnesses*, Chichester: Wiley.

Dezwirek-Sas, L., Hurley, P., Austin, G. and Wolfe, D. (1991), *Reducing the system-induced trauma for child sexual abuse victims through court preparation, assessment and follow-up*, Ontario: London Family Court Clinic.

Dezwirek-Sas, L. (1992), 'Empowering child witnesses for sexual abuse prosecution', in H. Dent and R. Flin (eds) *Children as Witnesses*, Chichester: Wiley.

Eltringham, S. (1994), 'Guardian *ad litem* estimations of the extent of children's knowledge of court and the contribution of psychological perspective towards such estimates', unpublished MSc. thesis, University of Leeds.

Feber, D.J. (1985), 'Age of witness competency: cognitive correlates', Honours Thesis, Monash University, Victoria, Australia.

Flin, R. and Spencer, J.R. (1995), 'Annotation: children as witnesses - legal and psychological perspectives', *Journal of Child Psychology and Psychiatry*, 36(2), 171–89.

Flin, R.H., Stevenson, Y. and Davies, G. (1989), 'Children's knowledge of court proceedings', *British Journal of Psychology*, 80, 285–97.

Freshwater, K. and Aldridge, J. (1994), 'The knowledge and fears about court of child witnesses, school children and adults', *Child Abuse Review*, 3, 183–95.

Goodman, G.S. (1984), 'The child witnesses: conclusions and future directions for research and legal practice', *Journal of Social Issues*, 40, 166.

Goodman, G.S. and Reed, R. (1988), 'Age differences in eye-witnesses testimony', *Law and Human Behaviour*, 10, 317–32.

Harvey, W. (1991), 'Preparing children for testifying in court', in N. Bala, J.P. Hornick and R. Vogl (eds) *Canadian Child Welfare Law*, Toronto: Thompson.

Home Office (1989), *Report of the Home Office Advisory Group on Video Evidence*, Chairman Judge Thomas Pigot QC, London: Home Office.

Home Office and Department of Health (1992), *Memorandum of Good Practice on Video Recorded Interviews with Child Witnesses for Criminal Proceedings*, London: HMSO.

Irish Law Reform Commission (1989), *Consultation Paper on Child Sexual Abuse*, Dublin: Irish Law Reform Commission.

Joel-Esam, B. (1994), 'Preventing child abuse in the courtroom: evidence on commission', *Child Abuse Review*, 3, 231–3.

Kendall, P.C., Howard, B. and Epps, J. (1988), 'The anxious child: cognitive behavioural treatment strategies', *Behaviour Modification*, 12, 281–310.

Koeppen, A.J. (1974), 'Relaxation training for children', *Elementary School Guidance and Counselling*, October, 14–21.

Mellor, A.L. (1991), 'Documenting the experiences of professionals involved in work with child witnesses', unpublished research project as part of Masters Degree, Birmingham University.

Mellor A. and Dent, H. (1994), 'Preparation of the child witness for court', *Child Abuse Review*, 3, 165–76.

NSPCC/ChildLine (1993), *The Child Witness Pack*, London: NSPCC.

NSPCC/ChildLine (1994), 'Preparing Child Witnesses for Court: Training and Resource Guide' (in-house NSPCC publication), Leicester: NSPCC.

Payne, D.C. (1992), 'An investigation of the legal knowledge of children in England,' unpublished MSc Thesis, University of Leeds.

Plotnikoff, J. (1990a), 'Support and preparation of the child witness: whose responsibility?', *Journal of Law and Practice*, 1(2), 21–31.

Plotnikoff, J. (1990b), 'The child witness', *Childright*, 63, 9–12.

Plotnikoff, J. and Woolfson, R. (1995), 'The *child witness pack* - an evaluation',

Home Office Research and Statistic Department, Research Findings No. 29, London: HMSO.

Robertson, J. (1970), *Young Children in Hospital*, London: Tavistock.

Saywitz, K. (1989), 'Children's conceptions of the legal system: court is a place to play basketball', in S.J. Ceci, D.F. Ross and M.P. Toglia (eds) *Perspectives on Children's Testimony'*, New York: Springer-Verlag, 131–57.

Saywitz, K. (1995), 'Improving children's testimony: the question, the answer, and the environment', in M.S. Zaragoza, J.R. Graham, G.C.N. Hall, R. Hirschman and Y.S. Ben-Porath (eds) *Memory and Testimony in the Child Witness*, Thousand Oaks, Newbury Park, CA: Sage.

Sisterman-Keeney, K., Amacher, E. and Kastamakis, J.A. (1992), 'The Court Prep Group: A Vital Part of the Court Process', in H. Dent and R. Flin (eds) *Children as Witnesses*, Chichester: Wiley.

Snaith, P., Owens, D. and Kennedy, E. (1992), 'An outcome study of a brief anxiety management programme: anxiety control training', *Irish Journal of Psychological Medicine*, 9, 111–14.

Spencer, J. and Flin, R.H. (1993), *The Evidence of Children: The Law and the Psychology*, 2nd edn, London: Blackstone.

Spicer, D. (1994), 'Abuse by process', *Child Abuse Review*, 3, 159–63.

Varma, V.P. (1984), *Anxiety in Children*, London: Croom Helm.

Westcott, H.L. (1995), 'Children's experiences of being examined and cross-examined: the opportunity to be heard?', *Expert Evidence*, 4, 13–19.

Wilkinson, J. (1988), 'Context effects in children's event memory', in M. Grunberg, P. Morris and R. Sykes (eds) *Practical Aspects of Memory: Current research and issues*, Chichester: Wiley.

Yuille, J. (1990), 'Expert evidence by psychologists: sometime problematic and often premature', cited by Harvey, W. (1991) in N. Bala, J.P. Hornick and R. Vogl (eds) *Canadian Child Welfare Law*, Toronto: Thompson, 255.

11 Dilemmas and opportunities in training around the *Memorandum*

Enid Hendry and Jocelyn Jones

This chapter begins with a review of developments and key issues for training on the *Memorandum of Good Practice on Video Recorded Interviews with Child Witnesses for Criminal Proceedings* (Home Office, 1992). It goes on to argue that a central but often neglected issue to be addressed on joint training for those interviewing children who may have been abused, is the issue of oppression and power relations. The difficulties of integrating anti-oppressive practice in inter-agency training are considered, with an analysis of the factors contributing to this difficulty. Finally, a framework is offered for understanding and successfully addressing structural and interpersonal oppression in both the training context and in practice. The chapter concludes with concrete and practical examples of how this framework can be built into training.

Background to joint training

Joint training programmes for police and social workers began around 1988 in response to the events of Cleveland, the recommendations of the Butler-Sloss inquiry and the Home Office Circular 52/1988 which emphasised the value of joint training. The initial emphasis of these programmes was on developing mutual understanding and breaking down some of the barriers to working together.

The introduction of the *Memorandum* in 1992 led to a revision and extension of joint training programmes and a shift in emphasis towards more 'technical' and skills based training. The importance of training as a prerequisite for those carrying out investigative interviews was made clear by the *Memorandum*. Support and guidance was initially provided to trainers through circulars, briefings at Hendon Police College and the publication of the Open University training pack *Investigative Interviewing with Children* (Stainton Rogers and Worrel, 1993).

141

Key training issues emerging from practice and research

A series of research studies, summarised in *Child Protection: Messages from Research* (Department of Health, 1995), have provided an insight into investigative practice and the experience of those involved. Hallett (1995) has highlighted how the police have moved to centre stage in child protection investigations. Hallett found that, although at times strained, working relationships between police and social workers are judged to be good by those involved. At the same time, questions have been raised about whether too many cases are being treated as investigations and whether too many interviews with children are being videotaped.

Those responsible for *Memorandum* training are experiencing a number of dilemmas, some of which have been highlighted in studies of the implementation of the *Memorandum* by the Home Office (Davies et al., 1995) and by the Social Services Inspectorate (Holton and Bonnerjea, 1994).

The key emerging issues can be summarised as follows:

- *Who should be trained* to conduct *Memorandum* interviews, and in what numbers? Holton and Bonnerjea (1994: 12) found considerable variance in the number of social workers trained and concluded that there was 'a danger that too many will be trained to an inadequate standard and then acquire little operational experience'.

  Hallett (1995) identified that police officers had a tendency to take control and dominate interviews and that police officers were seen by some social workers as more skilled in the task. The extent to which this is due to lack of experience or to power differences and oppression will be considered later in the chapter.

- *What should be the content* of training? Should it focus solely on interviewing or should this be in the context of inquiry and investigation? The absence of an agreed core curriculum or specified learning outcomes means that decisions about what to include or exclude are made locally. This can lead to significant differences in the amount of attention paid, for example, to child development and the more child welfare-oriented aspects of training, as opposed to evidential requirements and criminal justice aspects.

- *What standards* should be expected of those who have been trained and of those providing the training? There is an absence of any nationally agreed standards for those undertaking this specialist work, which is perhaps surprising in the light of the initial emphasis given to the importance of having training programmes that can deliver the necessary level of 'skills and specialised expertise' (Home Office, 1992: 3).

Davies et al. (1995: 44) reported, 'a perceived need for national standards', which was unanimously endorsed by trainers at a conference held in Leicester in March 1996. Professor Graham Davies and his team at Leicester are now working on the development of a national training strategy and curriculum for police officers involved in interviewing. Although the current research, funded by the Home Office, focuses on the police, it could be extended to include social workers with Department of Health approval.

- A related issue is whether, and if so how, competence should be assessed following training. Holton and Bonnerjea (1994: 33), in their survey of 91 social services departments found 84 per cent had no formal assessment of competence following training.
- To what extent and by what means should *Memorandum* training address values and attitudes, issues of oppression and the specific needs of children arising from disability, race, language, sexuality and gender? Concentration appears to have been on addressing minority group needs through representation. Holton and Bonnerjea (1994: 35) found that 'two thirds of local authorities had trained staff from a variety of racial and ethnic backgrounds', and that there was much debate about whether those working with children with learning, physical or sensory disabilities, 'should themselves be trained in video interviewing skills, or whether trained child protection workers should co-interview with them'.

Holton and Bonnerjea (1994: 12) also described complaints from social workers in two out of the five authorities studied, that 'courses did not deal adequately with issues of race and gender, and they were worried about some of the attitudes displayed by police officers'.

A survey by Westcott and Davies (1996) of *Memorandum* training in Area Child Protection Committees (ACPCs), conducted in 1995, found that respondents considered anti-discriminatory practice to be one of the least successful aspects of joint investigative interview training programmes, for which they had responsibility. The majority of respondents to the survey were social workers.

Some of the issues identified above relate to policy and strategy, while others relate to the delivery of training programmes. They pose considerable challenges to ACPCs and to those trainers in the police and social services departments who carry responsibility for this area of work. The remainder of this chapter will focus primarily on the neglected and challenging area of oppression and anti-discriminatory practice in *Memorandum* training.

Oppression – a central but neglected issue in *Memorandum* training

We will begin by defining oppression and considering why, and in what way, it can be seen as a central requirement to developing the expertise needed for conducting interviews with child witnesses. We will then move on to consider the reasons for its relative neglect in training programmes.

Oppression derives from the Latin *opprimere* which means 'to press on, to press against'. It implies being squashed out of shape, the use of force, being related to as an object or stereotype rather than as a human being (Phillipson, 1992). Oppression is concerned with power relationships and the abuse of power at both an individual and structural level, and as such, it is central to an understanding of all forms of child abuse. It also affects the nature of personal and professional relationships, including the co-working relationships of interviewers and of co-facilitators on a training programme. At a structural level, it influences decision making, the allocation of privileges in social hierarchies and what, or who, may be included or excluded. Thus for those involved in investigative interviewing it permeates the entire process from initial disclosure to court, and beyond to the child's eventual emotional survival. It affects the degree to which the interviewers themselves may feel sufficiently supported in their workplace.

It also affects the way this area of practice is viewed. 'Child protection work can be devalued as not being proper police work (i.e. arresting burglars or drug dealers)' (Adams and Hendry, 1996), its low status being reflected in the names assigned to units in some Police Forces: 'Fanny Squad, Women and Wains, Nappy Squad' (Lloyd and Burman,1996).

As *Working Together* (Department of Health, 1991: 53), says, 'The aim of training is ... above all, to learn how to interview children who may have been badly abused by other adults in such a way as to encourage them to provide information, without further hurting them.' Children are more likely to be enabled to talk about their experiences if those interviewing them have a real appreciation of how power is used to oppress, harm and silence them, and how internalised oppression damages self-esteem, distorts children's sense of self-worth, and makes them vulnerable to self-blame. Interviewers need to be aware of how their own behaviour could be experienced as oppressive by children who have been badly abused and how this could lead them to be either unable to speak, or to be over-compliant and anxious to say what they think the interviewer wants to hear. Westcott (1993: 75) has identified how disabled children, because of experiences of rejection, may be susceptible to socially desirable responding: 'They may find it difficult to challenge the actions of a non-disabled adult interviewer who may have made an incorrect assumption or misinterpreted a child's response.'

There are additional factors that can silence or create barriers to communication for certain groups of children. These additional silencing factors can relate to gender, ethnicity and disability and to the differential impact of structural and internalised oppression. Creighton et al. (1993: 14), state, 'since white authority is often perceived as oppressive, black children may find it difficult to disclose abuse to a white social worker or police officer'. Westcott (1993: 73) in the same volume also notes how 'the adult's power vis-à-vis the child will underpin the interviewer–interviewee interaction within the interview. For example, white adult–black child, middle-class adult– working-class child, non-disabled adult–disabled child'.

As well as underpinning the interviewer–interviewee interaction, power relationships can influence the co-working partnerships between the interviewers. Power inequalities can affect how decisions are made about who takes the lead, how differences of opinion are resolved and the balance of attention paid to the child welfare and criminal justice aspects of an interview. There can be a reluctance to address power differences openly and this reluctance can lead to collusion and to avoidance of conflict and difference. Not only may such differences be seen at the level of the interview, but they permeate the entire process. When unresolved the agenda shifts from one firmly located in the child's best interest, to one which focuses on the power politics between individuals and the various agencies involved in child protection and criminal prosecution.

A neglected issue

Given the centrality of anti-oppressive practice to this aspect of child protection work, why is this a relatively neglected aspect of training programmes? How can we account for the perception of trainers and participants that this is one of the least successful aspects of training? The fact that the *Memorandum* gives relatively little attention to considerations of race, language, culture and disability in interviewing children and makes no explicit reference to the need to address power issues is obviously not insignificant. A number of additional contributory factors can be identified:

- *Crowded programmes and competing demands for inclusion.* In spite of courses having been extended to between eight and ten days in many cases, there is still considerable pressure on time and difficulty covering all the relevant areas of knowledge and skills required to meet *Memorandum* guidance. In the absence of national guidance on what needs to be covered and what learning outcomes should be delivered, police and social workers make their own priority decisions. Where there are competing demands, emphasis on technical aspects of the

Memorandum and their practice application can take precedence over process, attitudinal issues and theoretical concepts.

- *Oppression is seen as social work issue.* Westcott and Davies (1996: 11), in their survey of ACPCs' training on the *Memorandum* quote an interviewee who neatly sums up a common experience: 'The police perspective of exercises such as working with the strengths of black families, effects of oppression etc., is that "this isn't relevant to us ... it's very much the social work side". Their perspective is that generally "we don't have a problem with race".' Consideration of these issues can be dismissed as 'political correctness', unless very clearly related to practice and specifically to effective interviewing.

- *Difficulty of addressing the issue* successfully in inter-agency context. On any inter-agency training programme, personal, professional and organisational dimensions of difference add to the complexity of the training process. For example, police and social workers experience distinct processes of professional socialisation, which give a different weighting to reflective practice and consideration of power relationships. Organisational cultures differ starkly, with the police operating in a culture that can be characterised as male dominated, action oriented, and one where humour, sometimes of a racist and sexist nature, acts as a form of tension release and group bonding.

  These differences that relate to the distinct role expectations of the two professions, make tackling oppression problematic and challenging.

- *Risk of polarising police and social workers.* Because of the inherent differences identified above, putting power relationships on the training agenda can risk dividing course participants along agency lines. One of the authors has direct experience of black participants and female participants from the police being torn by loyalty to police colleagues, possibly by fear of the after effects and as a result feeling unable to contribute when issues of oppression are discussed. Social workers have been observed to group together, taking the 'moral high ground' and using any slip, in terms of acceptable language, to pounce on police, who go into 'flight or fight' mode of response. Fear of such polarisation can lead to avoidance of the subject, but whether addressed openly or not, the dynamic of oppression will have an influence on the process of the course itself, as well as on practice.

- *Different starting points and prior learning.* Most social workers will have had opportunities to develop their awareness of personal and structural oppression. They can be expected to be familiar with the concepts and language as a minimum, whereas this is much less likely to be the case for police participants, where training on issues of equality has been much less extensive. It is arguable that inter-agency specialist training on the *Memorandum* is not the place to begin the learning process.

Just as the above factors make it difficult to tackle oppression in the training context, they can also affect practice detrimentally. An example of the consequences of avoidance in practice is provided by Hallett (1995) whose research indicated that social workers sometimes avoided arranging strategy meetings for fear of losing control to the police.

A conceptual framework for understanding oppression

A conceptual framework (Jones and Olusola, 1993; Jones, 1993; 1994; Wilson and Jones, 1995) is offered as a way of thinking about and understanding oppression. This can help both trainers and practitioners to overcome the difficulties described above, of integrating this issue in both training and practice. The framework addresses the interlocking nature of oppression and helps remind us of the experience of 'the other', and of the way in which, while we may share some of the same dimensions of oppression, we will differ in others. This can assist in overcoming the potential for polarisation and blame, discussed earlier.

The framework presented below identifies dominant and subordinate groups in British society. It enables individuals to understand their own capacity to dominate, or to be victimised, depending on who they are relating to, whether it is a child, a colleague, a manager, a barrister or member of the judiciary (Figure 11.1). The authors invite readers to apply and adapt the framework to their own local situation, for example, in Northern Ireland sectarianism will need to be considered.

The framework can help practitioners to appreciate the powerlessness of young children who are expected to talk about their abuse when crushed and intimidated by the power of an abuser who may possess many of the dominant group characteristics. It helps recognition of the additional barriers to be overcome to enable a black or disabled child to speak out. It can also be used to look at power relations between interviewers and to recognise, for instance, how the relative powerlessness of a female social worker working with a male police officer can contribute to a failure to effectively challenge a decision that is not child centred.

Joint planning can be improved when police officers and social workers share an understanding of power issues and have a language and framework that assists communication. They can consider what action they can take to empower child witnesses, for instance, by giving them relatively small, but

Figure 11.1: A conceptual framework for understanding oppression

Division	Dominant group	Subordinate group
Race	White	Non-white and divisions within
Language	'Queen's English'	Non-English Regional
Religion	Christianity	Non-Christian or Fringe Christian and strongly held religious beliefs
Class	Social classes 1–3 Ownership of wealth	Social classes 4–5 Lack of wealth
Employment status	Professional/managerial	Unskilled workers Unwaged and unemployed people Children
Sexual orientation	Heterosexual	Homosexual Bi-sexual
Age	25–35 years	Children and young adults People 40+ years
Gender	Men	Women
Ability/health	Able-bodied Fit, slim Intellectual Those with access to better education	People with disabilities and learning difficulties. People with mental illness. Those without access to better education

significant choices in the interview, and with that, a measure of control. Interviewers can also be assisted to use their own power to act as strong advocates for the child they have interviewed, for example, in discussion with the Crown Prosecution Service.

Practical applications in the training context

Some concrete suggestions are made below for developing anti-oppressive practice through *Memorandum* training. These include ways in which the framework (see Figure 11.1) can be applied:

- *Co-working agreements* between trainers need to be established if they are to train together effectively. The framework can help them consider the nature of their power relationship and their experience of oppression, thus providing a starting point for considering the possible implications this has for them in training together. For instance, when a young black female trainer from social services was training with an older and very experienced white male trainer from the police on a *Memorandum* training programme the opportunities and risks this posed needed careful consideration. In the event it was found that participants tended to direct all their technical questions to the police trainer and to avoid eye contact with the social work trainer, sometimes appearing not to hear what she said. This provided a valuable 'live' opportunity for examining how power relationships can affect co-working in practice.
- *Before the course* it is important to establish what prior learning participants have had in relation to issues of equality and to identify what they need to learn in order to conduct video recorded interviews in an anti-oppressive manner. This information is unlikely to be obtained through a questionnaire and will probably require a semi-structured interview which can then lead to a pre-course study plan geared to individual needs. The framework described above can be used in these specific circumstances or as general pre-course reading to help establish a common starting point and to maximise use of time on the course.
- At the *beginning of the course* it is essential to create a sufficiently safe learning environment and an ethos that allows supportive constructive challenges of any oppressive behaviour on the course. A working agreement that acknowledges power differences in the group and establishes a principle of equal value and of treating each person with respect is now common practice on most inter-agency training. In addition, considering what might make it unsafe to address differences can

be helpful and can be facilitated by giving hypothetical examples of possible barriers.

- An early *introduction of the conceptual framework* on the course, can be followed by an applications exercise in which participants work together to identify the relevance of the concept to joint interviewing. One simple exercise would be to ask the group to consider the implications of the model a) for interviewing children and b) for co-working. An alternative would be to ask participants to identify the factors that silence children and what action they could take as interviewers to help overcome the silencing factor without compromising the evidential value of the interview. In doing this exercise they could make use of the framework.

- *Opportunity to analyse power relationships* in practice could be provided by use of case material from external sources or from the course participants' own material. External case examples or video material (e.g., Castle Hill documentary 'The Secret of Castle Hill', Yorkshire Television, 1991) can be analysed to find evidence of how power was used and its consequences. A more challenging approach would be to video a group task on the course where group members in their professional roles have to reach a consensus. By giving a tight time limit to the task, group power dynamics are likely to be more stark. The exercise can then be analysed to consider the different roles participants took, and to identify the power dynamics. It would be important to identify examples of collusion and avoidance of challenge as a result of anxiety about oppression, as this can lead to dangerous practice.

- *Case material* used for interview skills development can include children who are likely to experience multiple levels of oppression. Planning of the interview will then need to take account of the possible implications of this for the interview. Debriefs of interviews should include the extent to which anti-oppressive practice was achieved and how strengths could be further enhanced.

Conclusions and recommendations

At the beginning of the chapter a number of dilemmas faced by trainers were identified. These included who to train, what should be the content of programmes and their learning outcomes, whether the competence of those trained should be assessed and if so to what standards. Given the 'special blend of skills required' and 'the formidable job specification' for interviewers referred to in the *Memorandum*, it is vital to get national agreement on the standards for training on the *Memorandum*. Trainers can make a well-informed contribution to this work. The development of nationally agreed competence requirements with processes for assessment and accreditation of interviewers, would be an important step in raising standards of practice, provided the standards recognised the need for an understanding of power relationships and were jointly supported by the Home Office, the Department of Health and the Lord Chancellor's Department.

This chapter has indicated that there is room for improvement in the way current training addresses power relations, and has suggested a conceptual framework and some concrete ways in which this could be integrated into existing programmes.

An appreciation of power relationships is fundamental to effective child-centred *Memorandum* interviewing. Power can be used to ensure that children maintain silence, or conversely it may be used to empower them to speak and ultimately to survive their abusive experiences. If anti-oppressive practice in *Memorandum* interviews is to be developed, trainers need to be mandated and supported to include this potentially difficult area in their training programmes. Clarity from the relevant government departments about the desired learning outcomes of courses and the practice standards required, would support this.

Anti-oppressive practice is the foundation of good child protection work and of effective child-centred interviews with child witnesses. Creating an environment and a rapport for abused children to speak freely about their experiences, while at the same time meeting the requirements of the courts, requires skills of communication located within a clearly defined value base. However, it is not just at this level that power relationships need to be addressed, but also at the organisational level between agencies and among individuals at the various levels within agencies. If we are to work together successfully to promote the child's interests, then all professionals involved in child protection need to have an understanding of when their own or their agency's agenda takes over and the child's powerlessness is forgotten as adult needs predominate.

Acknowledgements

Particular thanks to the students on the 1993–94 Leicester Diploma in Child Protection Studies programme who developed Figure 11.1 as part of their coursework.

References

Adams, C. and Hendry, E. (1996), 'Challenges to police training on child protection', *Child Abuse Review*, 5, 70–2.

Birchall, E. (1992), *Working Together in Child Protection,* Stirling: University of Stirling.

Butler-Sloss, E. (1988), *Report of the Inquiry into Child Abuse in Cleveland,* London: HMSO.

Creighton, C., Wattam, C. and Gordon, R. (1993), 'Awareness of Child Abuse', in *The ABCD Pack : Abuse and Children who are Disabled,* Leicester: ABCD Consortium.

Davies, G., Wilson, C., Mitchell, R. and Milsom, J. (1995), *Videotaping Children's Evidence: An Evaluation,* London : Home Office.

Department of Health (1991), *Working Together under the Children Act 1989,* London: HMSO.

Department of Health (1995), *Messages from Research,* London: HMSO.

Hallett, C. (1995), *Inter-Agency Co-ordination in Child Protection,* London: HMSO.

Home Office and Department of Health (1992), *Memorandum of Good Practice on Video Recorded Interviews with Child Witnesses for Criminal Proceedings,* London: HMSO.

Holton, J. and Bonnerjea, L. (1994), *The Child, the Court and the Video: A Study of the Implementation of the Memorandum of Good Practice on Video, Interviewing of Child Witnesses,* London: Department of Health, Social Services Inspectorate.

Jones, J. and Olusola, M. (1993), 'Power and oppression in child sexual abuse', in K. Ekberg and P.E. Mjaavatn (eds), *Children at Risk: Selected Papers,* Trondheim: The Norwegian Centre for Child Research, 403–19.

Jones, J. (1993), 'Child abuse: developing a framework for understanding power relationships in practice', in H. Ferguson, R. Gilligan and R. Torode (eds) *Surviving Childhood Adversity: Issues for Policy and Practice,* Dublin: Social Studies Press, 76–89.

Jones, J. (1994), 'Child protection and anti-oppressive practice: the dynamics of partnership explored', *Early Child Development and Care,* 102, 101–13.

Lloyd, S. and Burman, M. (1996), 'Specialist police units and the joint investigation of child abuse', *Child Abuse Review,* 5, 4–17.

Phillipson, J. (1992), *Practising Equality: Women, Men and Social Work,* London: Central Council for Education and Training in Social Work.

Stainton Rogers, W. and Worrel, M. (1993), *Investigative Interviewing with Children,* Milton Keynes: Open University.

Westcott, H. and Davies, G. (1996), 'Memorandum Training in ACPCs: A Survey', *Journal of Practice and Staff Development,* 5(3), 48–64.

Westcott, H. (1993), 'Interviewing children in an investigative context', in *The ABCD Pack: Abuse and Children Who are Disabled,* Leicester: ABCD Consortium.

Wilson, K. and Jones, J. (1995), 'Specific issues in training for child protection practice.' In K. Wilson and A. James (eds) *The Child Protection Handbook,* London: Baillière Tindall, 506–27.

Yorkshire Television (1991), 'The Secret of Castle Hill', Leeds: First Tuesday Specials.

12 The *Memorandum*: quest for the impossible?

Sarah Nelson

When I first read the *Memorandum of Good Practice on Video Recorded Interviews with Child Witnesses for Criminal Proceedings* (Home Office, 1992), followed by the research evaluation of videotaping children's evidence (Davies et al., 1995) I found myself overwhelmed by powerful emotions about the *Memorandum*: frustration, anger, incredulity, a sense of injustice and futility, of wasted time and effort and resources. These were surprising reactions to a reasoned, meticulous, often sensible, well-intentioned official document by thoughtful and caring people. They seemed intemperate and unfair. But they have also, I suspect, afflicted other child-centred workers in sexual abuse, who feel at these times that the world of reason and reality is stood upon its head.

We react thus not because there is some special failing about the *Memorandum*, but because it reveals yet again an obsession with the evidence of children which repeatedly produces deeply flawed results. Our shelves are laden with well-funded research studies, evaluations, Law Commission reports, proposals for change and invitations to the latest conference. Inquiries costing millions of pounds, such as Lord Clyde's meticulous Report on Orkney (1992), make numerous recommendations about the interviewing of children, but none in 363 pages about the possible need to pursue remaining concerns about those particular, real children.

Here, we have a *Memorandum* about just one aspect of children's treatment in particular cases; not in both civil and criminal courts, but only in the latter; not as a potential substitute for all court examination, not for the vital cross-examination, but simply for the evidence-in-chief. On that one part of the Criminal Justice Act 1991 we have whole books, like this one; we have detailed and continuing evaluations, conferences and seminars.

In contrast, we search extremely hard to find studies and reports on the reliability of evidence given by suspected adult abusers, or proposals on how we might devise tests and approaches which better discerned truth from

155

falsehood, fact from fantasy. Fantasising is, of course, a weakness of children, not of paedophiles. Adults need no competency test to ensure they know the difference between truth and lies. Yet strangely, almost every week we see uncovered abuses which continued for years or decades, where respectable adults had assured us nothing was going on, and stigmatised children protested their sufferings in vain.

Prospective interviewers and other child protection staff must digest and remember 52 pages of the *Memorandum of Good Practice* on one segment of their conduct, in pursuit of a goal which, Davies et al. (1995) found, made no significant difference to the outcome of criminal trials.

Extraordinary or contradictory demands are made upon those adults whose job it is to listen to the voices of children. Subsection 2.3 of this *Memorandum* informs interviewers that before even questioning the child, they must assess that child's cognitive, linguistic, emotional, social, sexual, physical and other development; their concept of time and ideas about trust; their knowledge of sexuality, their cultural background, disabilities and articulacy, and their present state of mind. Professional help in doing this may be valuable (it certainly would be!) but the 'implications for delay in consulting other experts should be carefully weighed' (p. 9).

During the interview they should not go too fast, and they should not go too slowly. 'There will, of course, be cases where the child has experienced abuse over long periods and such accounts may take a considerable time to narrate' (Subsection 3.11, p. 17.) It is not the length of abuse history which takes a child time: it is how able they feel to speak of it at all. Questioners must explain the reason for the interview during the rapport stage – except that they should not refer to the alleged offence nor mention the substance of any previous disclosure. They should also make the impossible and absurd request: 'don't leave anything out'.

After stepping through these and numerous other hoops in the 52 pages with the children, they discover a mere fraction of these videotaped interviews ever reach court. Astonishingly, more than 14,012 were conducted by police between October 1992 and June 1993 alone (Association of Chief Police Officers, 1993); what is the total today? Finally, adults and children involved find themselves in a court forum. A forum where neither judges, prosecutors nor defence barristers have any compulsory training in interviewing children, where age-inappropriate language is frequently used, where intimidatory tactics have been noted, where young people with special needs are often disgracefully unprotected, and where the adversarial system itself relies crucially on forms of cross-examination which confuse and discredit prosecution witnesses. ('Only' [sic] 34 per cent of children in the Davies study were rated as being 'very unhappy' during cross-examination.) It is the very job of the good defence counsel to discredit such evidence.

It is not only unjust and ineffective, it borders on the farcical that our society makes these incredible demands on children and their interviewers in order to achieve 'court-reliable' evidence, while leaving almost untouched the words and behaviour of the most powerful, decisive actors in those courts. This is why we all risk collusion by accepting these lists of rules, by going along politely with them, apologising continually for our mistakes and trying ever harder to rectify them. How quickly would the legal system change, in contrast, if social workers, police, child psychiatrists and others said: 'Could you explain why there is one rule for us, and another for you? We will follow these innumerable Memoranda, we will bow to these innumerable criticisms, just as soon as you do likewise.'

How important to the conduct and outcome of trials are endless efforts to achieve the magic 'court-reliable interview', how important in contrast is the latitude given in cross-examination, or the fact that in the Davies study 97 per cent of judges, 82 per cent of prosecutors and 88 per cent of defence barristers were male (Davies et al., 1995)? How many resources are put into serious attempts to outlaw certain techniques in cross-examination, or to diversify the sex, age, race and class backgrounds of key actors in child abuse trials – in comparison with the resources poured into 'the problem' of children's evidence?

I do not believe any *Memorandum* on interviewing children in sexual abuse cases needs to be more than about 15 pages of clear, basic guidance; particularly on the dangers in certain forms of questioning, on the need for good technical quality in techniques such as videotaping, and on issues like confidentiality and storage. It seems to me far more helpful to give explicit guidance on child development than to demand an assessment of it: to explain, for instance, that younger children, even of school age, share very little of adults' concept of time, and may simply be unable to conceptualise when, or how long ago, events took place.

This in itself immediately introduces a major problem. Once you start conducting interviews according to the way children actually are, you undermine the basic assumptions on which your practice is based (see Chapter 5). When times and dates are so important in court, what if many children cannot deliver them? If the interview room setting and format (preferably under one hour) is actually the least likely setting and timescale within which traumatised children will reveal painful secret truths, does this foundation stone need to be discarded? If they are most likely to reveal truths gradually over months, to trusted adults who are not considered qualified interviewers, in places like bedrooms, beaches or buses which are not considered reliable, can the systems we have established to elicit truth be remotely on the right track? Are very different, highly imaginative techniques like Madge Bray's far more likely to elicit the truth (Bray, 1991)? And if many sexually molested children have already been terrified by repeated pornographic videotaping, is the very use of this equipment secondary abuse?

How far can we reform our current guidance on children's evidence, how far do we instead need to shift radically our whole approach and focus in sexual abuse cases? I believe we need to do the latter, and that the *Memorandum* is another example of the fact that millions of pounds, countless staff hours of training, endless wasted effort, and profound stress inflicted on children has been spent in pursuit of an unattainable goal.

That goal is to do adults' work for them: to achieve 'reliable', unassailable evidence from teenagers, children and even toddlers, which will by itself identify genuine sex abusers and have them convicted in court, or at least ensure the children are protected. Yet the ceaseless quest continues, despite case after publicised case collapsing (especially in organised abuse) as children retract their evidence or find their testimonies judged to be flawed. Why have such a small proportion of videotaped interviews actually been used in criminal courts, why at so many different stages of the process has the option not been taken? There will be several reasons, but a central one is likely to be a failure of perceived credibility: a credibility, that is, in the eyes of adults.

I would suggest this whole expensive quest for 'reliable' children's evidence is a chimera, which the dictionary defines as an 'impossible or foolish fancy'. It should be abandoned as not merely unworkable and unproductive, but immoral and unjustifiable. In no other criminal cases do we demand that 80 per cent or indeed 100 per cent of the burden of proof is placed on small children and vulnerable young people: we investigate adults, instead.

The enormous resources and staff hours spent by people in many professions should be radically redirected, so that children's testimony and their other statements routinely supply no more than about a third of evidence in sexual abuse cases. This in itself enormously reduces the stress placed on children, especially when their evidence is viewed and valued as a series of potentially helpful clues in identifying adult abusers, and in bringing them to justice. But this new approach also demands radical rethinking of our philosophies and principles (see also Chapter 9).

Redirection should go into building up skilled multidisciplinary techniques of investigating suspected adults, both openly and in undercover work; refining knowledge of medical clues; keeping track of known, often highly mobile, abusers, including those who regularly go abroad on holiday to abuse children in third world countries; pooling knowledge and information from vast international stockpiles of 'captured' child pornography; building up good profiles of how abusers operate, for instance from convicted offenders; training all professions, including the law, about various patterns of child sexual abuse, and using more expert witnesses; listening properly to, and acting on, information from adult survivors, mothers of sexually abused children, and the voluntary organisations who work with both. These lines of inquiry will do far more to establish the truth, to obtain convictions, to distinguish the falsely accused, and to identify the actual abuser when several adults are possible suspects (like a natural father, a lodger and a new stepfather).

However, some of these measures undoubtedly have civil liberties implications. The way to deal with that is to bring them into widespread public debate, improve security and confidentiality of information, and ensure any suspects have the right to know the general nature of evidence or suspicions about them.

Why is the quest for ultra-reliable children's evidence unattainable and unethical? I have already mentioned that the 'court-reliable' interview setting may be the most unnatural one in which children can reveal painful truths. Secondly, the way small children (or some learning-disabled children) talk, assemble thoughts, behave, or paint and draw their messages will always remain incomprehensible to many adults. Young children cannot change their natural development for our convenience.

Thirdly, it is simply impossible clearly to disentangle therapy from investigation work, as the best practitioners know. It is immoral and unsustainable to deny distressed and damaged children the therapy and support they urgently need in case this may 'contaminate' their court evidence. It makes a mockery of all this rhetoric in official guidance about the primacy of children's interests and well-being.

Fourthly, each time a new technique is created and widely used, it creates its own major problems. Video interviewing is a clear example of this. The existence of many thousands of interviews on video brings enormous difficulties about confidentiality, security, ownership, short- and long-term storage. When should they be kept, when destroyed? Does agreement to the initial interview signify consent to its repeated use, and to its minute analysis by professionals acting for the alleged abuser? How is consent gained to its use for training purposes and is this ever justified? Most disturbing of all, such videotapes may fall into the hands of those interested in watching or selling them for pornographic interest.

Likewise, each time a new technique is created, it tends to take on a life of its own in which the letter quickly becomes far more important than the spirit. This encourages nitpicking and semantic arguments, and creates continual new reasons why the evidence obtained cannot be used in court or is somehow not valid. Several points in evidence submitted to the Steering Group of the *Memorandum of Good Practice* by Hampshire County Council's child protection team illustrate this well (Lucas, 1994): many other practitioners will have their own examples. The team write:

> Our experience in both county and criminal courts so far would indicate that barristers often interpret the *Memorandum of Good Practice* as statute, rather than as guidelines.

It seems also that practice is not reflecting the intention of the *Memorandum*. In a recent investigation where two teenage girls were tied up, drugged, indecently assaulted and in one case raped and buggered, the defence reached agreement with the Crown Prosecution Service that the video (believed by both police and social services department to be evidentially sound) should not be allowed as evidence-in-chief. The reasoning seemed to be that the girls made no disclosure of having been sexually abused, and therefore the videos were inadmissible as evidence.

Clearly neither girl was able to disclose sexual abuse as they were unconscious at the time of the assult. Medical and subsequently forensic evidence supported the abuse prior to interview. Indeed, one girl was in intensive care for a period of time, and the video interviews clearly provided much supporting evidence.

This approach was also taken in another case where a 13 year-old girl with special needs waited two years to go to Court. The video was only permitted as evidence-in-chief following a combined police and social services department appeal to a pre-trial judge. The reason for refusing to allow it initially was that it was made prior to the *Memorandum of Good Practice*. (p. 3)

A fifth and vital point is that children's evidence is believable or unbelievable not through some timeless objective test, but through the existing state of *adults'* knowledge and understanding about different forms of abuse. This knowledge develops through time and experience. For instance, accounts once dismissed as ludicrous or fantastic are now seen as recognisable patterns of organised ritual abuse by many practitioners. Even then, however, they may still not be by many judges or prosecutors, as the collapse of many 'cult abuse' cases suggests (Nelson, 1995; Strathclyde Region Social Work Department, 1995).

My sixth point is that historically inherited, authoritarian attitudes to children, the power dynamics in sexual abuse, and the huge power and resource imbalance between children and adults – especially articulate, respectable males – has two significant consequences. It means abused children, already torn between conflicting loyalties, will always be particularly subject to pressure and intimidation to retract. It also means the most meticulously prepared evidence will continue being challenged successfully, on one point or another, by people who can afford skilled lawyers, psychologists and other 'expert witnesses' (sometimes known more derogatorily as the 'flying circus'). It will be so challenged whatever new Memoranda appear on our desks.

The (often pseudo-scientific) methods used to discredit will not necessarily be predictable, as we have seen in the sudden appearance of so-called 'false memory syndrome', or FMS. This has been widely used to try to discredit adults who allege abuse in childhood (especially through recalling repressed memories). The meticulous, rational, reasoned search for 'better' facts, methods and evidence is always likely to be undermined by political battles in sexual abuse, waged by very powerful interests in society in a continuing war of attrition. There is still great naivety among professionals, media and the public about this, and about the scale of manipulation involved.

This is a war, not a polite, dedicated search for the truth by educated people who must surely share our concerns at heart. Feminists are aware of this, not because they are extreme or irrational, but because they have watched over the years every advance made in the understanding of sexual abuse being countered and undermined (Faludi, 1992; Hester et al., 1996; MacLeod and Saraga, 1988; Nelson, 1987). If and when FMS is finally discredited, they know we will not wait long for the next theory to appear, in an oddly simultaneous way, in academic journals and on the pages of some of our 'quality' newspapers.

To say that children's evidence must receive a much lower priority in sexual abuse is not the same as saying children do not deserve every effort to make the presentation of their evidence possible, and as free of stress, trauma and delay as it can be.

It is important to make this point, especially since an influential lobby still believes giving evidence is all so terrible for children that it is better not to put them through it at all. This simply means countless cases collapse or never reach court. That does not assist abused children, many of whom want and need to have their experience validated through the court process. In any case children's rights and dignity must be respected and given greater priority. We cannot pontificate about the need to listen to children unless we practise what we preach. Therefore it is important for many professions to keep collaborating, to explore all possible means of reducing stress and intimidation in the presentation of their evidence. That includes looking very seriously at current techniques of cross-examination and at whether they could and should be replaced, for instance by studying the experience and practice of other countries (see Chapter 8).

It also means not throwing the baby out with the bathwater with regard to new techniques. More selective, limited and thoughtfully planned video-taped interviewing than exists at present clearly has many merits in child abuse cases. In particular, it greatly reduces trauma faced by children in having to repeat their stories endlessly to different officials. It can much assist the police in following up clues given about suspected adults. But it will not be much value in court unless it is actually used in court, rather than never reaching this forum in a majority of cases. And it will not itself significantly reduce children's stress and trauma in court unless other important features of our courts and our trials are reformed.

But while it is important to retain our determination to improve children's experience of giving evidence, I believe we also have to look very seriously at why even those who believe they support and campaign for children are still largely stuck in the same mental groove as those who accord children far less respect. Why can we not break out of this assumption that children's evidence must be central in sexual abuse cases, that it constantly needs to be refined and made more reliable? Unless we bring our implicit assumptions as adults to the surface and analyse them, we cannot move on in our practice.

I think we hide too much behind the obvious, practical reason that in these cases there are often no other witnesses whose evidence we can take. Consider another whole set of cases where similar claims are made about the difficulty of assembling evidence: rape and domestic violence. I think the main reasons these crimes have remained so overwhelmingly undercover, why there are so few charges and fewer convictions, is not a lack of witnesses. Rather, it is because of many assumptions and prejudices, only recently challenged, about the rights and 'natural' behaviour of women and men. These have come through in interrogations, cross-examinations, and judges' comments.

The search for material evidence or background investigation of the alleged offender has often taken second place to a battery of assumptions about women's sexual behaviour, their unreliability ('wives just withdraw the charges') or the obvious social respectability of the alleged perpetrator (Dobash and Dobash, 1979; Hoff, 1990; Yllo and Bograd, 1988). These assumptions and prejudices have also made many victims too fearful or ashamed even to come forward after the crime.

Children are also subject to a battery of assumptions. We would never go to such lengths or set up such elaborate procedures for improving their 'reliability' if we did not believe there was a significant problem in the first place about children being untruthful or fantasising. There is a huge disparity between the problem which gains all the attention – which, most research suggests, is small and manageable (Jones and McGraw, 1987) – and the problem of children not being believed when they speak the truth. As I noted, hardly a week passes without some publicised case where children have been abused in a school or residential home for years or decades, where their accounts were not believed. There *is* an enormous problem about adults telling lies, yet we never seem to learn this message from repeated proof of that.

In these situations too, some adults – notably mothers – are often treated as unreliable children or worse. This means people who may have vital evidence and may have spotted signs of abuse early on are not taken seriously, because of untested assumptions which have passed into professional myth. The most conspicuous one is that if mothers are or have been involved in custody or access disputes, their testimony is suspect because they may be claiming abuse out of spite or malice (Berliner et al., 1987; Hooper, 1992; Nelson, 1994). That becomes a self-fulfilling prophecy: their evidence is never seriously examined, so it is more likely to be found 'false', so the myth that these mothers tell lies is strengthened. These assumptions are based on historic beliefs about the deviousness and untrustworthiness of women as a sex, rather than on serious exploration of their evidence using detailed knowledge of child sexual abuse. Thus is vital evidence ignored or lost.

We also have to look hard at why it seems so much more difficult to put suspected adults under the microscope, at why alleged offenders are often barely questioned or investigated. Why is it easier to place repeated and traumatic burdens on children? One unpalatable possibility is that we can do this with little 'comeback' from the children. In contrast adults – especially middle-class ones – can make all kinds of trouble, litigation and stormy publicity. How often is the easy ride they receive due to lack of courage and will, not necessarily by practitioners but by those above them in the hierarchy? A radical shift of direction among all relevant professions – which takes in the legal profession as a vital component – also demands a strong shift in political will, a willingness to ride out storms and justify action publicly; and a refusal to identify emotionally with other adults as adults, if it is possible that they have betrayed children.

There are many ways of looking for and finding evidence in sexual abuse cases which do not depend on the testimony of children; but which do draw on and test clues in their statements, remarks or behaviour, and on other suggestive evidence (see Chapter 9). For instance, English police officers in drastically underfunded and understaffed investigation units (Davies, 1994) have had some remarkable successes through following up evidence from pornographic videos used by paedophile sex rings. By identifying adults and young people in some of these films, they have made many arrests and broken up a number of sex rings.There is also a great deal of 'hard evidence' in written material, like paeodophiles' diaries of abuse.

Thousands of child sex videos seized by police cannot even be scrutinised, because the work investigators do is not given resources or importance, yet these will yield invaluable evidence leading to charges and convictions.This is one example where a radical switch in funding and support would probably yield far more successful prosecutions of abusers than any amount of refinement of children's evidence.

Looking in detail at an alleged offender's history at work and in relationships, taking statements from witnesses to those, taking and looking impartially at accounts of a marriage history from both partners, again shifts the focus onto adults. Using detailed and increasing knowledge about how sex offenders behave, and the links between sexual abuse and domestic violence, can also yield many clues about the possibility of abuse, especially where competing adults have been suspected. Often even the simplest, strongest indicators are not followed up: did X take every opportunity to be alone with the child, was Y not even interested in spending time with her?

Other kinds of investigation raise sharper civil liberties issues: searching homes, workplaces, caravans or cars for pornography or other items used in abuse; conducting surveillance, tapping phones, opening mail, politely re-questioning accused adults several times. The first necessity is to admit that children's civil liberties have been countlessly abused. Then these things have to be brought into public debate. How far are such unusual investigations justified in what is a serious and highly damaging crime? What safeguards need to exist, especially when (as with telephone tapping) some organisations are extremely worried that abuses are already occurring, in different contexts from sexual abuse, on innocent members of the public? But the debate will never begin unless it is kick-started.

If we look back at a situation like 'the Orkney child abuse affair' or indeed other cases of alleged multiple abuse, we find there were numerous possible clues given early on, in allegations by children, about the activities and movements of named adults; about their cars or trailers, the clothes they wore, the places they went, the equipment they took or had in their houses, the social circles they moved in, and so on. In the Orkney case, these detailed allegations can be found (using initials not full names) early in the inquiry report text itself (Clyde, 1992). In the Nottingham multiple abuse case (Tate, 1991), which did produce convictions of 10 people in 1989, different children gave a good deal of description about several large houses they visited, and professionals disagreed strongly with each other about the importance of this testimony.

In many sex abuse cases, single or multiple, such details have not been investigated seriously, or where the attempt has been made there have been practical difficulties about surveillance. But repeatedly and rapidly the focus has shifted from these possible clues onto the reliability and mental state of the children giving evidence, and the motives or competence of professionals who support them. These last have become the focus of media attention, and of subsequent, costly inquiries.

Perhaps the day is overdue for us to spend less time, training and scarce resources in trying to be better child psychologists: perhaps we should adopt instead, unfashionably, the mentality of the detective. Switching our attention to investigating adults will not merely gain those who work for child protection a far greater degree of 'court-reliable' evidence. It will also help create a climate in which young people are treated with humanity, and offered the prospect of justice. Those aims must surely lie at the heart of 'child-centred practice'.

References

Association of Chief Police Officers (1993), *Survey of the use of videotaped interviews with child witnesses by police forces in England and Wales*, Cheltenham: Gloucester Constabulary.

Bray, M. and Boyle, S. (1991), *Poppies on the Rubbish Heap: Sexual Abuse, the Child's Voice*, Edinburgh: Canongate.

Clyde, Lord (1992), *The Report of the Inquiry into the Removal of Children from Orkney in February 1991*, Edinburgh: HMSO.

Corwin, D., Berliner, L., Goodman, G., Goodman, J. and White, S. (1987), 'Child sexual abuse and custody disputes: no easy answers', *Journal of Interpersonal Violence*, 2(1), March, 91–103.

Davies, G.,Wilson, C., Mitchell, M. and Milsom, J. (1995), *Videotaping Children's Evidence: An Evaluation*, Leicester: University of Leicester.

Davies, N. (1994), 'Red light for blue squad', *The Guardian*, 29 November.

Dobash, R.E. and Dobash, R.P. (1979), *Violence Against Wives*, New York: The Free Press.

Faludi, S. (1992), *Backlash*, London: Vintage.

Hester, M., Kelly, L. and Radford, J. (1996), *Women, Violence and Male Power*, Buckingham: Open University Press.

Hoff, L.A. (1990), *Battered Women as Survivors*, London: Routledge.

Hooper, C.A. (1992), *Mothers Surviving Sexual Abuse*, London: Tavistock/ Routledge.

Home Office and Department of Health (1992), *Memorandum of Good Practice on Video Recorded Interviews with Child Witnesses for Criminal Proceedings*, London: HMSO.

Jones, D. and McGraw, J.M. (1987), 'Reliable and fictitious accounts of sexual abuse to children', *Journal of Interpersonal Violence*, 2, 27.

Lucas, R. (1994), Letter to Steering Group of Memorandum of Good Practice, Hampshire County Council Child Protection Team, Town End House, PO Box 61, East Street, Havant PO9 1UB.

MacLeod, M. and Saraga, E. (1988), 'Challenging the orthodoxy: towards a feminist theory and practice', *Feminist Review*, 28, 16–55.

Nelson, S. (1995), 'Locking up Pandora's Box', *Scottish Child*, Edinburgh, April/May, 18–19.

Nelson, S. (1987), *Incest: Fact and Myth*, 2nd edn, Edinburgh: Stramullion.

Nelson, S. (1994), 'Catch-22 for mothers', *Community Care*, 14 April, 26–8.

Strathclyde Regional Council Social Work Department (1995), 'Response by Director of Social Work: Ayrshire Children', 22 March.

Tate, T. (1991), *Children for the Devil*, London: Methuen.

Yllo, K. and Bograd, M. (eds) (1988), *Feminist Perspectives on Wife Abuse*, London: Sage.

13 The *Memorandum*: considering a conundrum

Helen Westcott and Jocelyn Jones

A 'conundrum' may be defined as a hard and puzzling question, and as the various chapters of this book have shown, the *Memorandum* is most certainly a challenging and puzzling document. Perhaps this is why such a variety of perspectives have been represented in preceding chapters, and why the *Memorandum* succeeds in eliciting some powerful and emotive responses. This probably also explains why, having deliberately set out to offer a wide-ranging assessment of the *Memorandum* in this book, we now find ourselves in the difficult position of trying to draw out common themes and sensible arguments in a closing review. Instead of trying to rationalise this difficulty, however, we have chosen to highlight it at the very beginning of our chapter, for we are beginning to believe that previous attempts to 'rationalise' or simplify the *Memorandum* may have contributed to the conundrum that it poses. The debate will and must continue, if children's rights to protection and to justice are to be achieved.

Protecting children

We must be very clear at the outset that children have a right to protection from abuse. What is less clear, however, is how, and how successfully, the *Memorandum* contributes to that protection. Furthermore, it has been suggested that, rather than protecting them, the *Memorandum* itself compounds the powerlessness and abuse of children (e.g. Chapters 5 and 12). The *Memorandum* unequivocally states that it is consistent and compatible with *Working Together* (Department of Health, 1991), and thus it aims to protect children. The *Memorandum*'s foreword notes:

> the interests of justice and the interests of the child are not alternatives. Children have a right to justice and their evidence is essential if society is to protect their

interests and deal effectively with those who would harm them (Home Office, 1992, p. 1).

Yet the assumption that promoting children's right to justice equates with promoting their protection is mistaken – as is the assumption that promoting children's right to justice equates inevitably with requiring their appearance in court (see Chapters 8, 9 and 12). Indeed, in reviewing the *Memorandum*, it is apparent that its implementation has generally increased the difficulties facing practitioners debating how best to protect the children with whom they are concerned. The consequences for these practitioners in terms of confusion about their role and personal stress are considerable (Chapters 2 and 11).

Presumably, the *Memorandum* was intended to protect children by increasing the numbers of children successfully giving evidence in court trials, and thus increasing the number of convictions of perpetrators. From the available evidence, however, it is not clear that this intended outcome is occurring (Chapter 1; Holton and Bonnerjea, 1994). At this point it is perhaps useful to take a step back and consider a preliminary review of the advantages and disadvantages of the current system for dealing with children's evidence, of which the *Memorandum* is a part. These are shown in Table 13.1.

For every advantage there is at least one and usually more disadvantages, even in this preliminary review. The final point in Table 13.1 is perhaps the most telling in terms of children's protection, especially when we consider that there exist no mechanisms for examining the outcomes for children suspected of being abused (i.e. were they protected, did their welfare improve?), nor seeing whether their involvement in the child protection and criminal justice systems had any impact upon such outcomes. Indeed the general lack of statistical information relating to child witnesses is lamentable (see, for example, Plotnikoff and Woolfson, 1995). We are still left, then, with the thorny issue of how it is that the *Memorandum* promotes the *protection* of children from abuse, while acknowledging from (Table 13.1) that the reforms of which it is a part may serve to promote children's *welfare* in certain respects.

A right to justice

The *Memorandum* appropriately emphasises that children have the right to justice, but there are hints in Table 13.1 that it has yet to meet this aim too. What does a child's right to justice consist of? The right to give their own account in court proceedings? The right to see more perpetrators convicted of offences against children? It seems that in neither of these respects has the *Memorandum* been particularly influential.

A host of commentators have argued how adversarial criminal justice

Table 13.1: Advantages and disadvantages of the current system for dealing with children's evidence

Advantages	Disadvantages
Children can give evidence-in-chief via videotaped interview	It is unclear what criteria should be applied to determine when to interview and which children should be interviewed, with major implications for resources and children's welfare
	Although videotaped interviews are not negatively influencing court outcomes, they do not appear to be positively affecting them either
	Research has shown a reluctance to use videotaped interviews in court, and children are often denied the use of their videotaped evidence at the last minute
	Children still have to be cross-examined live in court
The *Memorandum* gives helpful guidance on how to interview children, and promotes good practice in interviewing	The *Memorandum*'s guidance is being interpreted as binding by many defence barristers and judges in court cases, with alternative approaches open to criticism
	The *Memorandum*'s guidance is best suited to older children who are more willing and able to give a detailed verbal account of their experiences. It is not sufficiently inclusive of very young, disabled and black children, nor children who are less articulate. Such children may require an approach designed with their specific needs in mind

Table 13.1: continued

Advantages	Disadvantages
	The *Memorandum*'s guidance does not apply to, and indeed is widely ignored by, barristers and judges interviewing children in court
The *Memorandum* promotes inter-agency cooperation	The *Memorandum* was implemented without sufficient resources for inter-agency training and development of coordinated practice
	There is insufficient guidance (and no national standard) as to what core elements *Memorandum* training should consist of
	There remains tension between police and social services over who should lead the interview
Children should be able to receive therapy prior to giving evidence	This expectation has been subjected to differences in local practice, with some children still being denied therapy post-interview before court
The *Child Witness Pack* (NSPCC/ChildLine, 1993) has been developed to prepare children for court	The *Child Witness Pack* has been implemented without sufficient resources and without any stipulation of responsibility, so that many children do not receive any preparation for court whatsoever
	Professionals who have prepared children for court are typically excluded from supporting them in the court- or videolink-room

Table 13.1: concluded

Advantages	Disadvantages
	Preparation is often portrayed by defence barristers as coaching in an attempt to discredit child witnesses
The *Memorandum* and related Criminal Justice Act reforms emphasise the value of listening to children's accounts of their experiences	The way the *Memorandum* and reforms have been interpreted in practice, both in videotaped interviews and in court, does not afford children the opportunity to give their accounts in ways that are meaningful to them

systems serve to undermine children's ability to give an account of their experiences in court (e.g. Spencer and Flin, 1993), with defence barristers in particular seemingly able to behave towards child witnesses with impunity. Westcott (1995) has highlighted three ways in which children are denied justice in court: through intimidation, repeated accusations of falsehood, and lawyers' questioning style. Linking these issues to the UN Convention on the Rights of the Child (United Nations, 1992), and particularly Article 12, p. 17, she concludes,

> Studying children's experiences of examination and cross-examination, it is often difficult to see how trials can have anything to do with seeking justice or genuine fact-finding. Certainly, intimidating children, repeatedly calling them liars and speaking to them in language they cannot understand can hardly enhance this process – no 'opportunity to be heard' here ... the cross-examination of children needs to be regulated ... Simply abusing a position of power in relation to children, as is permitted at present, should not be countenanced.

A number of the authors in this book would no doubt support this view. It is too harsh to lay this blame on the *Memorandum* itself, however, for cross-examination and the treatment of children in court lie beyond its remit. Nevertheless, such failings are symptomatic of the ambivalent view of children and their evidence held by adults – especially those in authority (see Chapters 4 and 12) – and of the rather half-hearted, piecemeal approach to reform which has subsequently resulted.

The speculative second 'component' of a right to justice given above – the right to see more perpetrators convicted – has also not been supported by the evaluation of the *Memorandum* and Criminal Justice Act 1991 (Chapter 1). Care is required in interpreting the evaluation's statistics, since it is necessary to consider not only videotaped interviews shown in court, but also video-tapes which lead to guilty pleas earlier in the process. However, as Davies et al. (1995: 34) state, 'Once guilty pleas were excluded, proportionally, there was no difference between the rates of acquittal for the videotape trials com-pared to all trials involving child witnesses.' They then go on to report that there was no significant increase in the number of guilty pleas submitted in videotaped cases, despite a slight trend in this direction (49 per cent in appli-cations to use videotape compared to 44 per cent in cases where no applica-tion was made). Again, the lack of comprehensive, coordinated statistics collated by government departments is lamentable, and prevents an analysis of other issues which may be relevant, such as whether there has been a general increase in the number of children coming to courts as witnesses since the introduction of videotaped evidence-in-chief. However, implemen-tation of the Criminal Justice Act 1991 and the *Memorandum* does not appear to have made a marked impact on outcomes for child witnesses, making us question whether it can be said to be achieving justice for children. What *is* apparent is the need for more open and honest debate about what 'justice for children' is actually taken to mean by the different actors involved in child protection and criminal justice.

At this point it is necessary to remind ourselves that children and families themselves have their own perspectives and aspirations in this respect. Although, as 'detached' professionals we may have increasing concerns about the viability and desirability of children's participation in the criminal justice system as it stands, we must not forget recent research evidence high-lighting how much some children and carers want to see perpetrators taken to court, even if it entails children giving evidence themselves (Prior et al., 1994; Sharland et al., 1993). Children and carers are 'actors' too, and their perspectives are central to any debate.

The way ahead

Following such a pessimistic review of the *Memorandum*, we must, then, con-front the awkward question of how to go forward. It is perhaps worth first remembering that the relevant Criminal Justice Acts and the *Memorandum* have conferred some improvements for children. In attempting to answer this question we are drawn to the rather inevitable conclusion that there are three possible routes forward: first, to 'tinker' with the existing system; secondly, to introduce more substantial changes to the existing system (e.g. implementation of the whole Pigot scheme), and thirdly, to overhaul the way child abuse cases are prosecuted. None of these options is without significant resource implications.

Tinkering with the system

Many of the preceding authors and other commentators (e.g. Murray, 1995; Plotnikoff and Woolfson, 1995; Spencer and Flin, 1993) have suggested ways in which the current system may be enhanced by essentially minor changes offering major improvements. These can be grouped according to whether they are required pre-, post- or during the trial.

Pre-trial, there should be comprehensive preparation of the child witness as well as support and preparation of non-abusive carers (see Chapter 10). Where necessary, the child should receive therapy without negative implications for their credibility at trial. There should be appropriate pre-trial hearings at which decisions made about the trial (such as the use of videotaped evidence and/or videolinks) become *binding*. The delays which are apparently endemic in the criminal justice system should be tackled aggressively by the relevant authorities and personnel. The failure to curb the delays between an allegation being made and the child appearing in court, and the fact that such delays are increasing inspite of the government's speedy progress policy, represent yet another damning indictment of policy and practice in this area. Plotnikoff and Woolfson (1995) provide a detailed analysis and recommendations for the effective management of child abuse prosecutions and reduction of delays.

A number of specific revisions to the *Memorandum* are also necessary, such as improved guidance on pre-interview practice and criteria for conducting a videotaped interview, guidance on large-scale investigations such as suspected organised abuse networks, and better advice on the planning, timing and general conduct of the interview. The manner in which the *Memorandum* serves to disempower child witnesses has been highlighted, and a more positive revision could indicate greater involvement of children and exercise of choice by them over key decisions in these three areas. A revised *Memorandum* should also consider the particular requirements of very young, highly traumatised, black and disabled children in more detail. Crucially, it needs also to refer to the interviewing process in court. Guidance (and standards) for barristers and judges could either be incorporated in the *Memorandum* itself (see Chapter 3) or in a complementary document. Linked to this last point, a national approach to training issues in relation to child witnesses is urgently needed, with specified competence requirements for investigative interviewers (e.g. social workers and police officers), barristers and judges.

At court, judges must be prepared to take on a more active role (Westcott, 1995) to ensure a trial that is fair both to the defendant and to the child witness. As the Director of Public Prosecutions has commented (Mills, 1994: 14): 'We should not permit a system where decisions about guilt or innocence are based not on truth of the allegations being made but on the witnesses' fortitude when giving evidence.' A number of other measures are also available, many of which have already been successfully implemented in Scotland (Murray, 1995). For example, there should be better waiting facilities at courthouses, with rooms exclusively available for use by the child witness and his or her supporters. Special, small court-rooms should be used, with appropriate amplification systems and alternative arrangements for seating the child witness with his or her support person. Judges and barristers should remove their wigs and gowns if the child desires, and the public gallery should always be cleared in cases of child sexual abuse, or other cases where it appears that the defendants' supporters are intimidating the child.

Post-trial appropriate support and/or counselling should be given to the child and other supporters and family members. The child should have the verdict and sentence (where guilty verdicts have been returned) explained, and should be informed as to the likely next steps in the process. Children and their carers should also be informed when an incarcerated offender is released back into their community, either on parole or on completing their sentence.

More substantial reforms to the current system

Spencer and Flin (1993) provide a comprehensive account of the background to the Pigot Report (Home Office, 1989), as well as persuasive arguments for the implementation of the full Pigot proposals, and we will not repeat them here except to note the benefits to the child of giving all their evidence before trial. Simply, the child does not have to suffer the prolonged delays and suspension of their normal life. They can receive therapy 'without any strings' and can move forward to put their experiences behind them as best they can. They do not have to undergo the traumatic experience of a court appearance, and particularly live cross-examination. In endorsing the benefits of such a system, however, we should remember the minority of children who actively desire to give their evidence live in court. As Cashmore has suggested in her evaluation of videolinks in Australia (Cashmore and De Haas, 1992), the success of such technology may lie more in the choice that is given to the child (i.e. to use or not use the link) rather than simply the technology itself. We should also be mindful of the caution issued by Plotnikoff and Woolfson (1995), who argue that if pre-recorded videotaped cross-examination was introduced on a discretionary basis, then it would probably remain ineffective. Speaking of the existing reforms introduced by the Criminal Justice Act 1991, they conclude from their research:

While reforms were intended to apply to a wide range of child victims and witnesses, the exercise of judicial discretion has operated to undermine the broad purpose of legislative intent because many judges have interpreted the new provisions rigidly and restrictively. [We] came across a number of examples of what the Director of Public Prosecutions has condemned as 'justice by geography'. (p. 96)

One of the measures suggested by Plotnikoff and Woolfson to improve children's situations is the development of independent advocates for criminal courts, similar to the role of the guardian *ad litem* in civil proceedings. As O'Neill has shown in Chapter 4, there is already much overlap between the two jurisdictions where children are suspected abuse victims. Formalising the role and duties of an advocate in cases where children are witnesses may be another avenue by which the child's experience may be improved, especially if that advocate was able to intervene during the trial itself, for example during cross-examination, to alert the judge if the child did not understand the counsel's questions, or if intimidatory tactics were being employed of which the judge was not aware. Westcott (1995) discusses cases where the videolink was being misused by defence counsel, but the supporter with the child was unable to inform the judge.

Finally, with respect to more substantial reforms such as these, or any overhaul (see below), Spencer (Chapter 8) has reminded us of the importance of keeping an international frame of reference, especially any potential breaches of the European Convention on Human Rights.

An overhaul of the system

In their earlier chapters, Liz Davies (Chapter 9) and Sarah Nelson (Chapter 12) have already suggested approaches to the prosecution of child witnesses which place a different emphasis on the child's evidence. Without repeating in detail the substance of their chapters, the point is made by both that much greater attention should be placed upon investigating the perpetrators of sexual abuse, making more use of traditional police methods, with less emphasis on the child's testimony. This is not to say that children's evidence should not be heard by the courts, rather that children themselves should not, and do not have to be, the exclusive source of evidence in the majority of cases. Similar points have been made by Spence and Wilson in their analysis of American *Team Investigation of Child Sexual Abuse* (1994), and indeed during the time this book was being written, the Home Secretary announced new proposals for curbing the activities of sexual offenders (see 'Howard plans paedophile curbs', *The Guardian*, 13 June 1996). These include some of the initiatives suggested by Davies and Nelson in earlier chapters, such as requiring sexual offenders to register with the police every time they move home, and to ban them for life from work with children.

Critiques like those of Davies and Nelson (Chapters 9 and 12) offer an exciting challenge in a field where despair and weariness are easily experienced by all concerned. Despite earlier assurances by the Government that the reforms for child witnesses would be reviewed following relevant evaluations, and similar sentiments expressed during various questions in the House of Commons regarding a revision of the *Memorandum* (see Plotnikoff and Woolfson, 1995, for a review), there has been a notable lack of activity in these respects. Although there have been some improvements for children as a result of the recent Criminal Justice Acts, these have not gone far enough. It really *is* time that the relevant government departments in a position to review – honestly – the whole range of evidence relating to children as witnesses did so. As part of such a review alternatives should be explored. Spencer has provided an international overview in this volume and elsewhere (Spencer and Flin, 1993; Spencer et al., 1990), and other approaches could include the development of a helpline and drop-in service like ChildLine to provide children with completely confidential advice on possible lines of action, and the likely consequences of a disclosure. We must challenge the notion that in any other system than the current one the defendant's rights are subjugated, and be open to positive alternatives which prioritise children's welfare. However, a review of children's evidence will only succeed if its recommendations are acted upon. We must learn from the fate of the Pigot report (Home Office, 1989).

Conclusion: empowering children

Power is an essential dynamic in the fields of child protection and criminal justice which must be addressed whichever route to change is adopted. This book is perhaps unusual in that so many chapters have explicitly considered power issues and the related concept of oppression – a concept which is noticeably absent from many discussions of children's evidence and the *Memorandum* (and indeed from the *Memorandum* itself). Children's rights to protection and justice hinge on them being empowered, which translates at a basic level into giving children as many choices and as much control as is possible, given their circumstances and individual capabilities. Gupta and Marchant and Page have already reminded us how particularly important this is for black and disabled children. However, it is equally the case that those professionals whose role it is specifically to promote children's welfare through their empowerment – social workers and guardians *ad litem* – will only be able to fulfil their role if they themselves feel sufficiently strong and supported (see Chapters 4 and 11).

Social workers in particular are subject to the prevailing political climate, and the current Children Act 'section 17 versus section 47' debate is not noticeably assisting them nor children and families. In brief, this debate centres around the degree to which, under the Children Act 1989, social workers are responsible for helping 'children in need' or undertaking child protection investigations, with the suggestion that an unhealthy emphasis on the latter has hindered the former (Department of Health, 1995). The manner in which this 'debate' has developed, however, and especially the failure to consider or offer additional resources, leaves much to be desired. With respect to child witnesses, this debate puts social workers in a particular paradox, since they will be expected to make more crucial decisions earlier on about whether a criminal investigation is likely (and hence whether to pursue a *Memorandum* interview). Yet they are simultaneously under greater pressure to withdraw from the 'heavy end' of investigative work. Thus, for example, there are discussions as to whether generic or specialist social workers should be trained to undertake *Memorandum* interviews (e.g. Westcott and Davies, 1996). As Brownlow and Waller have discussed, the social work profession is struggling with this issue, and while the profession is striving to define its own role its capacity to help children is severely impaired.

Feminist writers have distinguished between 'power over' and 'power to (act)' (Frye, 1983; Jagger, 1983). 'Power over' refers to power inequalities at a macro or structural level, while 'power to act' applies at an interpersonal level, and refers to an individual's ability to resist oppression in a specific situation. The degree to which an individual has the power to act in any given situation is controlled by the actions of the other(s) who are in a position of power. This distinction is reflected in the discussion above, and provides a framework for understanding our use of the term 'empowering' children. Attempts to empower individual children will be limited by the extent to which the criminal justice system *disempowers* child witnesses generally and maintains powerful adult authority figures such as judges and barristers. Thus we must concern ourselves with the fundamental power dynamics involved when considering children's evidence and the *Memorandum*, child protection and criminal justice.

If we now turn to our previous discussion of the way ahead, it becomes obvious that attempts to 'tinker' with the existing system of obtaining evidence from children will inevitably be of limited success if the underlying structural issues are not simultaneously tackled. So, although we would call for the changes detailed above under this heading to be instigated immediately, by themselves these measures will not go far enough to shift from the prevailing adult agenda to that of the child. What is also required is a new model of child protection and criminal justice, as hinted at by Cross et al. (1995). These authors have called for a 'new understanding of prosecution of child sexual abuse ... that takes into account the large proportion of cases that do not go to trial' (Cross et al., 1995: 1431). Further, with this new understanding, research would look at outcomes for children and families involved in the whole range of legal and child protection interventions, not just those that result in trials. Policy-makers and practitioners would devote more attention to the initial investigation and alternatives to prosecution (see Cross et al., 1995: 1441).

We support such a view, and suggest that only collaboration between policy-makers, practitioners and researchers may lead to a new model of child protection and criminal justice, and appropriate reforms for children as witnesses. What is essential is that this collaboration is based on an open acknowledgement of existing power relationships, that it happens *now*, and that a coherent and comprehensive plan for change is developed. Children deserve more than the disjointed, piecemeal approach that has dominated this field to date.

References

Cashmore, J. and De Haas, N. (1992), *The Use of Closed-Circuit Television for Child Witnesses in the ACT*, A Report for the Australian Law Reform Commission and the Australian Capital Territory Magistrates Court, Canberra, Australian Capital Territory.

Cross, T.P., Whitcomb, D. and De Vos, E. (1995), 'Criminal justice outcomes of prosecution of child sexual abuse: A case flow analysis', *Child Abuse & Neglect*, 19, 1431–42.

Davies, G., Wilson, C., Mitchell, R. and Milsom, J. (1995), *Videotaping Children's Evidence: An Evaluation*, London: Home Office.

Department of Health (1991), *Working Together Under the Children Act 1989: A Guide to Arrangements for Inter-Agency Cooperation for the Protection of Children from Abuse*, London: HMSO.

Department of Health (1995), *Child Protection: Messages from Research*, London: HMSO.

Frye, M. (1983), *The Politics of Reality: Essays in Feminist Theory*, New York: The Crossing Press.

Holton, J. and Bonnerjea, L. (1994), *The Child, the Court and the Video: A Study of the Implementation of the Memorandum of Good Practice on Video Interviewing of Child Witnesses*, London: Department of Health Social Services Inspectorate.

Home Office (1989), *The Report of the Advisory Group on Video Evidence*, Chairman Judge Thomas Pigot QC, London: Home Office.

Home Office and Department of Health (1992), *Memorandum of Good Practice on Video Recorded Interviews with Child Witnesses for Criminal Proceedings*, London: HMSO.

Jagger, A.M. (1983), *Feminist Politics and Human Nature*, Brighton: Harvester Press.

Mills, B. (1994), *Tom Sargant Memorial Lecture 'Justice for all – all for justice'*, London: JUSTICE.

Murray, K. (1995), *Live Television Link: An Evaluation of its Use by Child Witnesses in Scottish Criminal Trials*, Edinburgh: HMSO.

NSPCC/ChildLine (1993), *The Child Witness Pack*, London: NSPCC.

Plotnikoff, J. and Woolfson, R. (1995), *Prosecuting Child Abuse: An Evaluation of the Government's Speedy Progress Policy*, London: Blackstone.

Prior, V., Lynch, M. and Glaser, D. (1994), *Messages from Children: Children's Evaluations of the Professional Response to Child Sexual Abuse*, London: NCH Action for Children.

Sharland, E., Seal, H., Croucher, M., Aldgate, J. and Jones, D.P.H. (1993), *Professional Intervention in Child Sexual Abuse: Report to the Department of Health*, Oxford: University of Oxford Department of Applied Social Studies.

Spence, D. and Wilson, C. (1994), *Team Investigation of Child Sexual Abuse: The Uneasy Alliance*, Newbury Park, CA: Sage.

Spencer, J.R. and Flin, R.H. (1993), *The Evidence of Children: The Law and the Psychology*, London: Blackstone.

Spencer, J.R., Nicholson, G., Flin, R.H. and Bull, R. (1990), *Children's Evidence in Legal Proceedings: An International Perspective*, Cambridge: Law Faculty, Cambridge University.

United Nations (1992), *Convention on the Rights of the Child Adopted by the General Assembly of the United Nations on 20 November 1989*, London: HMSO.

Westcott, H.L. (1995), 'Children's experiences of being examined and cross-examined: the opportunity to be heard?', *Expert Evidence*, 4, 13–19.

Westcott, H.L. and Davies, G.M. (1996), 'Memorandum training in ACPCs: a survey', *Journal of Practice and Staff Development*, 5 (3), 48–64.

Index

181